Raise a

✝

Signal

compiled by
Hyla Stuntz Converse

RAISE A SIGNAL

On a bare hill raise a signal

ISAIAH 13:2

RAISE A SIGNAL

*GOD'S ACTION AND
THE CHURCH'S TASK IN
LATIN AMERICA TODAY*

A SYMPOSIUM COMPILED BY

HYLA STUNTZ CONVERSE

1344

FRIENDSHIP PRESS
NEW YORK
1961

CONTENTS

FOREWORD

Raise a signal! The white truce flag, the fire alarm, the starter's gun are signals. The lanterns in the belfry of the Old North Church signaled to Paul Revere, and a revolution that was ready began to move. In the remote reaches of the Himalayas, bonfires on the barren heights may signal of an avalanche disaster or an approaching tax collector. Two Negro students in Greensboro, N. C., asked for lunch counter service; their action proved to be a signal, and a waiting river of revolt against injustice and indignity began to flow.

In the Biblical account that is the source of the title of this book, the people of Israel had been defeated and taken as slaves, forced laborers to Babylonia. God seemed either to have been defeated or to have withdrawn from the world. But the signal on the bare hill (Isaiah 13:2) would proclaim that God was still sovereign in his world. And because he was, the raising of the signal would prove to be the initial event in the people's deliverance from exile and slavery. Now God was beginning to bring down the tyrants and to deliver and gather his repentant people. The prophet's signal *said* that the Sovereign God was on the move to accomplish his purpose for men, and the signal *was the beginning* of God's momentous actions.

In much the same way the Christian community, the church, has been called forth by God in Jesus Christ to be a sign, to raise a signal, to say and start something.

Where is God's sovereign hand at work today, breaking down and lifting up? And what is the church called upon to say, and say with its life, in response to God's work? God always works through particular events, historic movements, particular people. If we want to understand God's work in the world and thus discover what is to be our own obedience, we have to struggle with these questions together, within our own national and cultural situation. But also we have to meet our Christian brother whose different national position may lead him to understand God's work in different ways, whether in ways that confirm and encourage us or in ways that reveal to us our self-deception and blindness. This is true for him also. We need desperately today to come into dialogue with our Christian brothers in other parts of this revolutionary world.

This book is written to us from Latin America by fellow Christians deeply engaged in trying faithfully to raise a signal on a bare hill. They write out of particular situations and experiences. You will find that they disagree with one another at times. You will also find that there are some things so important in Latin America today that two or three writers deal with the same subject, each from his own perspective. One point that is worthy of note is the importance of theology to all these writers—persons caught up in pressing everyday problems in a very dynamic, often overwhelming situation.

We have in no way tried to harmonize views or edit out these significant restatements. For we are engaged here in listening. Whether this becomes the beginning of dialogue depends on whether we allow ourselves to be spoken to by our fellow Christians in Latin America, both about their situation and about our own; whether we open ourselves to God's action toward us in this encounter.

Raise a Signal is the fourth study book of this kind on a particular area of the world. The others have been *Recon-*

ciliation and Renewal in Japan, by Masao Takenaka; *Multitudes in the Valley,* by Denis Baly, about the Middle East; *The Halting Kingdom,* by John and Rena Karefa-Smart, about Africa. This series has been planned jointly by the Literature and Study Committee of the Commission on World Mission of the National Student Christian Federation and the Commission on Missionary Education of the National Council of the Churches of Christ in the U.S.A. A fifth book, Peter Berger's *The Noise of Solemn Assemblies,* about the United States, will be available through NSCF in the summer of 1961.

Like the other books in this series, *Raise a Signal* is closely related to the concerns expressed in the World Student Christian Federation emphasis on the Life and Mission of the Church. It centers attention on the life and mission of the church in Latin America. In addition, most of the writers have been closely related to work being done under the WSCF emphasis. Others have been related to similar work being carried on under the World Council of Churches. Thus, *Raise a Signal* has added relevance for us as we try to discern God's demands upon the church's life as it engages in his mission in the United States.

I should especially like to thank the authors who contributed to this book. They accepted their assignments on rather short notice and when already burdened with prior commitments. They have struggled faithfully with us by correspondence against the barriers and uncertainties of distance and language. And theirs is the credit for the response which I am sure this book will call forth.

February, 1961

HYLA STUNTZ CONVERSE
LITERATURE AND STUDY DEPARTMENT
COMMISSION ON WORLD MISSION
NATIONAL STUDENT CHRISTIAN FEDERATION

BEATRIZ

MELANO COUCH

We were living under Perón's tyranny. People all around were selling or renting their souls and the idealistic student generation of Argentina was working underground against the oppression. I was a student at the University of Buenos Aires. I invited students to our home where we could think freely together about the questions being raised all about us. The communists had their answers as did other secular groups. The Roman Catholics had theirs. But what would a truly Protestant witness be? I began to feel more and more the need for a thorough theological preparation to help myself and others find some answers.

Scholarships at Tift College and later at Princeton Theological Seminary in the United States made possible the education I needed. My sense of urgency was sharpened by the Athens, Ohio, conference of the Student Volunteer Movement in 1955 and by participation in a venture it inspired, an ecumenical mission team in Mexico. A year of travel to university campuses on behalf of the SVM brought me into close relationship with students from many lands. During an unforgettable journey to Rangoon and the conference there of the World Student Christian Federation in 1959, I came into a new understanding of the oneness of Christ's church and its staggering mission.

In 1957, Richard Couch, a young American minister, and I were married. While he completed his graduate studies, we thought and searched for clarity about our future ministry. Gradually we sensed that both of us were being called to serve in that land whose vast need had originally spurred me on. In February, 1959, we were sent by the United Presbyterian Church in the U.S.A. to serve on the faculty of Union Theological Seminary in Buenos Aires.

As time has passed we have become increasingly aware of the fact that the greatest challenge of all is to be willing to discover in everyday experience the deep meaning of the washing of each other's feet, even of those who refuse to be served. We have come to feel that only as this becomes the pattern of our ministry may we begin to discover the joy of being witness to and participant in the miracle of redemption.

10

INTRODUCTION

by Beatriz Melano Couch

The smallness of our planet is one of those blunt facts that refuse to wait neutrally until we choose to contemplate them. We live next door to neighbors we have not particularly noticed before—neighbors who could in a quick turn of events become enemies. There is, therefore, a distinct strain of self-interest in the new emphasis upon getting to know more thoroughly the language, culture, and customs of the other nations of the world.

There is, however, or should be an added dimension in the significance the contemporary Christian puts upon his need to understand nations beyond his own. Alongside the striking smallness of our planet, another fact has been pushing in upon our consciousness. It is the growing sense of oneness in mission among many of the scattered branches of Christ's church. It has become increasingly clear that this is not just another movement toward consolidation, but that it belongs to the very nature of the church. God has drawn together a dispersed people. "Now in Christ Jesus you who once were far off have been brought near . . . you are no longer strangers and sojourners, but you are fellow citizens with the saints and members of the household of God." (Eph. 2:13, 19)

If this new understanding of the church is to be really operative in its life, each national church must be viewed as called to the discipline of truly confronting its brethren in other lands, of coming to know them and letting itself be

11

known, and of trying to discover the best way for this new awareness to take concrete form.

As this ecumenical encounter has begun to take place, it has become clear to many that part of the miracle of the church is that the "unsearchable riches of Christ" can never be fully contained in any one church tradition or in any one ethnic type. Each succeeds perhaps in grasping clearly one or two particular dimensions of the gospel. There is thus in a certain real sense a Spanish Christ and a "Christ of the Indian Road," an Oriental Christ and an Anglo-Saxon Christ. But the full miracle of the church is not apparent until each of the national, cultural, and racial vessels within the ecumenical community learns to pour into the others the gracious riches God has given it and to receive from them. Only thus may we begin to approach something of "the measure of the stature of the fullness of Christ." (Eph. 4:13)

We always have these riches in the earthen vessels of culture, historical tradition, and racial idiosyncrasy. It is only into such vessels that God pours his redemptive riches. The riches are always vastly greater than the vessel in which they are contained; but, in the ministry of sharing that we must exercise together in the ecumenical community, each person must have a certain basic interest in, and respect for, the earthen vessels of others. This means the sometimes painful process of genuine understanding.

One of the ironies of history is that, in spite of a whole host of factors that would seem to dispose North America and South America to a natural neighborliness, each continent has been more intimately associated with other parts of the world. The ties that bind North America to countries in Europe, and even to the Far East, have been much stronger and more influential than the ties that bind her to the continent to the south. In Latin America, ties of sentiment, language, heritage, and culture are much stronger with the Old World, even with the non-Latin countries of the Old

World, than with her New World neighbors to the north. Probably the most tragic result of this has been that, rather than viewing each other as colaborers in the colossal New World enterprise of mastering the wilderness, assuring the common man a high level of material well-being, and giving political reality to man's thirst for liberty, Americans north and south have viewed one another through a series of sadly distorted images.

Distorted Images of Latin Americans

One of the most prevalent false images maintained by North Americans with regard to "those other Americans" is that they form a more or less homogeneous block of very similar countries, inhabited essentially by the same people, by one ethnic and cultural group. It is crucial for a proper understanding of Latin America to see it as made up of some twenty distinct nations, each with a number of vigorous, ethnologically different groups, boiling together in what may be seen as another version of the melting-pot phenomenon. In some countries, such as Mexico and Peru, there is a rich and powerful Indian heritage; in others, such as Argentina, the population is almost entirely the result of large European immigrations (Italian, British, German, Swiss, Polish, and Spanish). The cultural influences of Latin America are many and varied. Geography, an important conditioning factor for economy and culture, ranges from the sparse, high valleys of the Andes to the impenetrable Amazonian jungles. Even the casual visitor to Latin America soon discovers how ridiculously oversimplified it is to lump together such vastly different countries as Colombia and Argentina, Bolivia, Honduras, and Chile.

Another widely accepted but false image refers to the personality of the Latin American. The reader will probably not find it difficult to locate in his imagination the picture of a short, simple, dark-skinned man in colorful dress, possibly on horseback and with a large sombrero, singing gay and colorful songs to the strumming of his guitar; or that of the similarly dark-skinned female counterpart, complete with long, attractively colored dress, dangling earrings, and a suggestively sultry expression, ready at any moment to burst into a vibrant, rhythmic dance. This image is false, not because such people cannot be found, but because they are not nearly as representative as is normally assumed.

The Latin American is by no means necessarily dark-skinned. All Latin American countries have significant segments of the population that are as purely Caucasian as any ethnic groupings in North America. Although it is true that the general level of education and culture is low in Latin America as compared to North America, the cultured man is generally much more thoroughly cultured than his North American counterpart; and there is a whole treasury of Spanish culture—literature, music, painting, philosophy— that is unfortunately veiled to the average North American because only in rare instances is he sufficiently conversant with the Spanish language and history to appreciate it.

There is perhaps an even more important dimension of the Latin soul that escapes those who give in to the false image of the guitar-strumming gentleman and his attractive partner: the dimension of chronic sadness. The most exportable music and dancing has undoubtedly been the gay, the colorful, and the rhythmic; but the really characteristic Latin music has an inescapable tone of sadness. Paraguayan music tends to portray the melancholy of its persecuted Indian race. There is a deliberate, doleful, even anguished note in much of the folk music from northern Argentina. Even the dances from that region often portray the timidity and restraint of a reserved, perhaps inhibited people. In much of Brazil's music, even that which is superficially more gay, there is a pervasive element of sadness, probably of Negro origin. Latin America is a land of magnificent dreams and tragic failures. Her music bears witness to both.

A further false image of the Latin American pictures him as a hot-tempered revolutionary, given to violence, periodically amusing himself with another "week-end revolution." How many times North Americans have hastened to ask me, after learning that I was an Argentinean, whether we were "having a revolution down there, too?" Yes! We *are* in revolution down here! But North Americans will miss completely the significance of this, if they dismiss our revolution with a smile because they identify it with the immature and temperamental forms that it sometimes takes. We are a continent in search of its soul. After centuries of existence under the yoke of authoritarian rule in church and state, we are groping towards a real democracy; but the heritage of authoritarianism makes this at times a most precarious experiment. In a continent originally subdued by the unholy wedding of the cross and the sword, the way of force and violence is firmly rooted in tradition and can be rejected only in the course of a long and difficult struggle.

There are legitimate national ambitions behind the political upheavals of Latin America. Memories of the days when many Latin American countries were only functions of the economic and political interests of foreign powers and foreign companies are still strong. There is a jealous watchfulness over the national independence and sovereignty of each nation. Perhaps more than anything else there is a deep human need for recognition. Nations need to feel that they have an important destiny in the concert of the nations, that their voices are heard when they speak. Nothing could be more misleading than to dismiss as communist all manifestations of nationalism or criticism of North America by Latin Americans.

A final distorted image is that which pictures the Latin American as lazy and backward, not even interested in exerting himself for his own welfare. There can be no doubt that one of the strongest impressions received by the North

American executive is just this. A technical consultant in an Argentinian steel plant recently lamented, "In the United States everything is sacrificed to get the job done and quickly; here the job itself proceeds at a creeping pace because everything else looms so large in the picture—personalities, pride, status, bureaucracy, selfish interests."

There can be no doubt that involved here is a serious fault in the Latin make-up: a general inability to lose oneself in co-operative effort. But it is a serious mistake to interpret this as mere laziness or inertia. The North American should recall that his nation's whole history, from hazardous frontier days on, has obliged him to take a thoroughly practical approach to things and has taught him the disciplines of the job. The South American tends to orient himself much more to personalities than to plans or programs. Spain, more than anything else, was a mother of great men. South American history is to a great extent the history of great personalities who were able to incarnate a cause and thus stimulate a people to action. This is eminently true of the continent's great *liberatadores:* San Martín, Bolívar, O'Higgins. What impresses the North American as laziness and inefficiency is something that goes much deeper into the heritage of the Latin type. This trait can lead to dangerous extremes; yet in contrast the North American devotion to the job tends toward the "corporation man."

Distorted Images of North Americans

The Latin American in turn views his North American brothers through images. These are just as convincing to him and just as dangerously distorted. He tends to view all North Americans as shrewd, hard-driving businessmen, interested in turning to their own economic advantage their underdeveloped southern neighbors. This image is easily used and amplified by communist propaganda, but it does not originate there; it is the product of contacts with North

Americans whose conduct and attitude have made them their country's least desirable representatives abroad. Rather fatally for Americans north and south, it too often happens that those North Americans least prepared to understand and relate positively with Latin Americans are the ones who go there in the largest numbers and that those best prepared to understand stay home.

It serves no purpose to try to excuse the abuses that have been committed in the history of North American investment in South America or the interventions of the United States to protect its economic interests, but it is essential for those on both sides of the fence to recognize one economic fact of life that largely explains the course of events. The plain fact is that North America has been for decades a highly developed industrial area in the midst of others rather seriously underdeveloped. This has made her naturally a source of capital and made her neighbors a most natural place for investment. Without anyone's especially wanting it that way or seeking to create such a state of affairs, North America has gradually become the hub of an economic sphere, while her neighbors have become increasingly dependent upon her. That this situation has not been the product of organized malice toward Latin America should be clear to the informed Latin American. That the Latin's resentment at having to assume a dependent role is far more than a response to communist propaganda should be clear to the North American.

Strangely, a further distorted image concerning the North American seems to be a direct contradiction of the exploiter image, even though given equal credence. It is the image of the naïve, uninformed, trusting, fair-haired American! "Naïve" and "trusting" because he treats people often with confidence and a complete lack of caution or suspicion, generally expecting fair treatment in return. "Uninformed" because of the generally limited scope of his information, being confined normally to knowledge of his own field and incomplete information even about his own culture.

Both judgments have some basis in fact, but they are easily exaggerated because of certain cultural idiosyncrasies of the Latin himself. Much in his own culture has led him to view as smart the shrewd, quick person who knows how to seek his own advantage. *"El vivo vive del sonso y el sonso de su trabajo."* "The smart fellow lives on the fool and the fool lives on his work." The Latin American, therefore, finds it difficult to appreciate the general air of confidence and mutual trust with which things are usually done in a North American setting.

Nor is the Latin normally aware of the differences in educational theory that help explain what appear to be crucial gaps in the North American's information. Whereas the educated Latin has generally had a broadly humanistic training, with studies in many fields and often less intensive study in any one field, the North American has been educated in a primarily pragmatic system, with fewer broad cultural subjects and a more thorough training in his particular professional field. There is surely room to discuss the merits and demerits of either system, but it is hardly justifiable to describe as ignorant or uninformed one whose training has simply been different.

The Church North and South

With regard to the work of the church, perhaps the difference that impresses one most between the northern and southern halves of this hemisphere is that between "order" and "ardor," as someone has characterized it. Although it is by no means universally true in Latin America, there is a certain tendency towards an enthusiastic, passionate understanding of the gospel and propagation of it. The Latin American Protestant, or Evangelical as we say, usually accepted the gospel in the midst of an environment that was openly or tacitly hostile to it. Thus it has been for him an utterly new experience of freedom and religious vitality, one that he has had to defend from criticism and misunderstanding on all sides. In some cases this has resulted in his being called upon to die for his faith. But the resulting enthusiasm with which he expresses and defends his faith has meant sometimes a marked propensity towards schism and a chronic inability to bear any meaningful impact on the life of society around him.

His North American brother, on the other hand, has left on the church the mark of his natural capacity for order and organization. A most impressive amount of good work around the world has been undertaken because the North American churches, with a distinct strain of Puritan industry, have known how to mobilize and dedicate their resources to vast enterprises. Even the vital matter of evangelism has tended to assume all the dimensions of big business! But the very efficiency of this organization has sometimes seemed to render passionate religious conviction unnecessary. Where today is there a North American Christian who could seriously count himself ready to suffer and die for Christ?

Is it not possible that God would speak to us through the way in which our chief virtues, north and south, seem to complement one another? Ought not all of us to come to grasp the importance of having both an "ordered" and an "ardored" discipleship?

What Can We Do?

If we ask ourselves as Christians how these false images and differences bear upon the life of the church or how we are to be obedient to Christ within the context of misunderstanding and prejudice, we should be careful not to provide too easy an answer. It is beyond a doubt true that deeper than all the distortions there is the one Lord, the one faith, the one baptism. It is this that unites us. We should not allow this conviction, however, to obscure for us the fact that we are still children of our age, influenced more than we know by our own culture, by national and racial prejudices, by the falsifications of propaganda. The following suggestions may help indicate the direction of the road of obedience.

In the first place, we must take the necessary pains to know one another in our own cultural settings. This is far more than mere accumulation of data. It is the difficult process of exposing ourselves to our brother just as we are, accepting him just as he is, and giving serious consideration to what he may think of us. Real understanding can begin only in such a context of mutual openness and acceptance. But this is part of what Christian love means concretely; it is a love that always involves sacrifice and risk.

In the second place, there must be a clear awareness that the gospel as it is proclaimed in North America has a particular cultural context, upon which it has had a formative influence but with which it is by no means identical. This cultural context can never become an export item, sent along with the gospel as if it were an essential part of it. The gospel must partly find and partly form anew a cultural context if it is to be truly effective in the lands where it is proclaimed; and this means one context in the mountains of Bolivia, another in the jungles of Brazil, still another in Caracas.

In the third place, the church in North America, every bit as much as the diplomat and the investor, must take realistic and intelligent account of the revolutionary situation in Latin America if there is to be a meaningful encounter with the people. It is just as disastrous for the North American church as for secular agencies to dismiss the phenomenon of revolution in Latin America as essentially an alien factor, merely an expression of the disorderly elements in society.

The chapters that follow will explore the ways in which the church in Latin America must discover faithfully its responsibility in the midst of rapid social change and revolution. They will point up the significance of the contemporary spiritual vacuum and the utterly crucial role that the church in Latin America may play as a cohesive community in the midst of a host of centrifugal forces. They will show the need for the church to break out of a limiting middle-class mold into the currents of unrest all about it, so that instead of remaining a spiritual elite removed from the world's ferment, it may discover the tent-like existence of the prophetic community, obediently on the march to serve God in the world.

A final, but by no means less important, indication of the road of obedience along which the church both in North and South America must walk, if a true sense of unity in mission is to be found, has to do with missionary personnel and personal contacts. There are perhaps few developments that would contribute more to a genuine partnership in obedience between Christians on these two continents than that a generation of capable and committed young people should sense the peculiarly demanding and challenging situation in revolutionary Latin America.

In many ways the situation throughout Latin America is particularly ripe for a forthright and sensitive presentation of the gospel. Alongside a certain suspicion towards Christianity, there is a new kind of openness and hunger, perhaps nowhere better summarized than in the words of a Chilean student quoted by John A. Mackay: "I have for some time been in revolt. But a man cannot be a rebel forever, even if he wants to . . . I need a faith. Do you think I can ever get a faith?"

There is a variety of other ways in which the personal factor may help contribute to understanding and to community in mission. There is no substitute for personal confrontation in the process of getting to know others; no amount of theoretical knowledge about other peoples and their way of life is an adequate substitute here. Here again the traditional predisposition towards Europe and Asia has meant that the church in North America has neglected some of the finest and most effective means at its disposal for contact with Latin America. Only an occasional ecumenical caravan has been undertaken south of the Rio Grande. Summer work camps have been undertaken on a very meager scale.

The Junior Year Abroad program, either in its merely academic or its church-sponsored form, has been far more thoroughly exploited in Europe, Asia, and Africa than in the countries of Latin America. It is well to remember in this connection that Latin America has a number of very fine universities, usually patterned on the European academic system. A very profitable Junior Year Abroad could be spent in many of these centers of learning.

Possibilities for personal confrontation have been increased in recent years by the practice, now followed by several North American denominations, of sending short-term missionaries to various countries. The assignment is usually for college or seminary graduates and may be for two or three years.

An almost entirely new field is that of internships. In the case of seminary students who have mastered the language and who have a sense of vocation about the church's mission on cross-cultural frontiers, a year's internship with a Latin American church could be of great benefit—for them, for the church served, and for mutual understanding in the ecumenical community. A stimulating new program is that of the United Presbyterian Church in the U.S.A., called the Frontier Internship Program, in which college and seminary graduates will spend two years in a specific foreign country, such as those of Latin America, rendering service in frontier situations.

That more and more legitimate opportunities for such contacts must be sought became clear to me during a recent summer with an ecumenical caravan in Mexico. Europeans,

North Americans, and South Americans participated in the project. In spite of all that should have recommended the team members to brother Christians all across Mexico, it became clear that some Mexican Christians harbored serious misgivings with respect to the North American members of the team. That fellow Latins, whom they readily accepted, were deeply involved in a co-operative work with these suspect brethren from the north became the point of contact for a new understanding on all sides. In the course of sharing in worship, Bible study, and evangelistic efforts, the points of suspicion and misunderstanding melted with a consistency that baffled explanation, and a genuine human encounter became possible. As matters stand at the moment, this experience was a highly isolated case, but we venture to believe that it may indicate a pattern for the future.

VALDO

GALLAND

I am Uruguayan. In 1916 my father was sent from Switzerland to South America to do student work through the YMCA and in relation to the World Student Christian Federation. I was born in 1920 in Colonia Valdense, a settlement of Waldensians that began with a migration from Northern Italy a century ago. I was baptized in the Waldensian Church and am still a member.

My high school years were spent in Buenos Aires at Colegio Ward, the missionary school of the Methodists and Disciples. I studied theology from 1940 to 1944 in Geneva, Switzerland.

From 1945 to 1949 I served as lay pastor of the Protestant French-speaking community of Buenos Aires. At various times I served on the board of Union Theological Seminary of Buenos Aires, on the Editorial Committee of *Predicator Evangélico* (a magazine for pastors and lay preachers), and as chairman of the Ecumenical Commission of the Federation of Evangelical Churches. I was also active in the Student Christian Movement.

In 1949 my wife and I went to the United States, and I studied for a Master's degree in theology at Princeton Seminary. The following year I continued graduate studies in Geneva. In 1951 I received the *Licence de Théologie* and was ordained.

By the middle of 1951 I joined the staff of the WSCF. My particular responsibility was to organize the first WSCF Leadership Training Course in Latin America, which took place near São Paulo in 1952. The following year I was reappointed Latin American Secretary of the Federation. During the next three years, I visited all the Latin American countries, helping SCMs to develop their work or helping people to start student work.

At the Tutzing WSCF General Committee in 1956, I was appointed Associate General Secretary, which meant that my base was again in Geneva. I was still involved—with my successor, Mauricio Lopez—in the organizing of the Leadership Training Course for Central America in 1956 and for Mexico in 1957, and the South American Bible Study Leaders Training Course in Brazil in 1959. On March 1, 1961, I succeeded Philippe Maury as General Secretary of the WSCF.

CHAPTER ONE

GOD'S PRESENT WORK IN LATIN AMERICA

by Valdo Galland

Latin America Yesterday and Today

It is said again and again that Latin America finds itself in the midst of upheaval, turmoil, turbulence, and agitation. Revolutions, military coups, the overnight change of presidents, the rise and overthrow of dictators, outrageous nationalistic manifestations, huge meetings of roaring mobs, and violent speeches by political leaders seem to be daily bread for the twenty Latin American republics. But beyond this fact, the question is worth asking: How did this turbulence originate? History teaches us that it did not begin recently—within the last ten, twenty, or thirty years—but that it has been going on ever since political independence.

In the same year that the last Spanish troops were defeated (1826), Simon Bolívar, one of the main leaders of independence, called a meeting in Panama with the purpose of bringing about Latin American unity. The failure of the conference was like a signal for further splitting up of the former Spanish colonies. What was Great Colombia now broke into Colombia, Venezuela, and Ecuador; the United Provinces of Central America split up into several small countries; the viceroyalty of New Castille was divided into Peru and Chile; the United Provinces of Rio de la Plata gave birth to four nations: Argentina, Bolivia, Paraguay, and Uruguay. Only the Portuguese colony was able to retain its unity, thus becoming, under the name of Brazil, the largest Latin American country.

Chaos and anarchy have characterized the beginnings of nearly all these countries. The *caudillos,* regional political leaders, often with separatist tendencies, played an important role in the early stage. The number of crises undergone by the majority of the countries is almost incredible. Before the end of the nineteenth century there were fifty internal political crises in Argentina; in Peru, between 1821 and 1871, there were forty revolutions, and in 1834 no less than eight different governments; Ecuador had twelve constitutions in eighty years; Venezuela, eleven constitutions and fifty-two revolutions up until 1900; Colombia, seven constitutions and seventy revolutions in the same period. And this is by no means a complete list! In addition, six wars were fought between Latin American countries in the period from 1825 to 1935.

It is easy to laugh at the instability of Latin American governments. But before laughing we should perhaps consider the question: Is Latin American political instability the cause of its economic backwardness or the result? If the latter, are we going to say that the whole responsibility of economic backwardness lies only with the Latin Americans themselves? Has the rest of the Western world clean hands in this matter?

We cannot disregard the fact that the economic life of the colonial period was disastrous for the colonies, which were considered simply a reservoir of cheap raw materials and an area where industrial products of the mother country could be sold at high prices. After independence, colonialist exploitation was replaced by foreign economic imperialism. France and England, who had generously helped the revolutionaries, were well aware that Latin American independence would not only weaken the Spanish enemy but would also open to them new, advantageous market places. Both countries provided large amounts of capital for the exploitation of the natural resources, assuring themselves of substantial returns and economic control of their strategic investments.

The defense of these interests called for many acts of intervention, of which the Franco-Mexican war is one of the most outstanding. But soon this European imperialism ran headlong into North American imperialism, which, in a way, started when the United States provided help to Mexico to defeat France. The Texas declaration of independence from Mexico; the United States protectorate over Cuba, Haiti, and the Dominican Republic; the United States armed intervention during the Mexican revolution; the establishment, by the United States, of Panama as an independent country at the time of the canal's construction; the more or less indirect United States help to maintain this or that government in power or to throw it down—all these have been acts of intervention to defend important economic interests.

But only out of blindness could it be alleged that Latin American economic backwardness is due merely to external factors. We cannot overlook Latin American responsibility for the present situation. We have to be aware, first of all, that political independence was largely the work of the creole aristocracy; that is, of the sons of Europeans born on Latin American soil. Inspired by the French revolution, the creoles fought for democratic ideals as well as for their own economic interests. In these circumstances, political and economic liberalism proved inadequate to deal with the new situation created by political independence. Soon the Latin American countries were governed by an aristocratic, conservative oligarchy, which, allied with foreign economic interests, prolonged the feudal situation of the colonial period.

Furthermore, the supremacy of the creole class has meant a tendency to think about all Latin American problems through a European perspective. This proclivity has been reinforced by the stream of European immigration, which, in fifty years, increased the population from six to eighteen millions. In many countries this influx meant the rise of a middle class that found expression in the Radical parties. When in power, the latter introduced some social reforms, which usually fell short of tackling the problems in a thoroughly indigenous way. In view of this predominant tendency to think in European terms, we should not be too surprised by the important role played in Latin American history by *caudillos* and dictators, who have generally been expressions of strong nationalistic feelings.

What Road Ahead?

Our century has seen many popular movements striving to support the interests of the masses. We may list among these the Mexican revolution, the Apra[1] movement of Haya de la Torre in Peru, the former Guatemalan government under presidents Arevalos and Arbenz, the Peronist movement in Argentina, the present Bolivian government, and, last but not least, the Cuban revolution led by Fidel Castro. Some of them, like the Apra movement, have never succeeded in getting into power; others, as for instance the Arbenz government, have been thrown down with the help of outside forces; others, like Peronism, have been unable when in power to avoid political corruption, which constitutes, alas, a long and solid tradition in Latin America. But the noticeable fact about these movements is that they have tried or are trying to take into account the conditions and demands of the masses without merely reproducing foreign patterns. They are, indeed, Latin American expressions of the social revolution that is sweeping over the whole world.

Without having gone thoroughly through a period of political democracy, Latin America has entered the period of social revolution where the aspirations of the masses, reinforced by a rapidly growing industrialization, have to be taken into account. Where is the road into the future? Old patterns of political life are still influential: nationalism and *caudillismo* (dictatorship) often adopting neofascist methods; capitalistic oligarchy, always ready to ally itself with foreign interests; democratic idealism, playing with ideas without much realism.

There is clearly a deep and urgent need for a social revolution that will bring both economic and political democracy —a "popular democracy" assuring bread, education, and freedom to all the people and not only to a privileged class.

Other chapters will deal more specifically with these questions, but it should be said here that this whole situation constitutes a favorable ground for communism, which, in spite of the reduced number of its adherents in Latin America, is no negligible force. The outlawing of the Communist party has never proved effective in stopping its growth. Hundreds of young Latin American intellectuals are getting university training in Eastern European countries. They come back to their homelands with great convictions and a sacrificial spirit. There is a moral force there that cannot be destroyed with weapons. The present real need for thoroughgoing social revolution provides a real opportunity for communism. And it will do so increasingly, as long as old-fashioned patterns of government perpetuate themselves, thanks to military force or the help of economic imperialism.

What is going to happen in Latin America in the near future? Can we Christians say anything about the present and the possible future of this vast area of more than 180 million inhabitants? We believe that Christ, who is the Lord of the whole world, is also the Lord of Latin America, that God reigns over the whole world and that Latin American history, also, is in his hands. Since we believe this, how does this conviction affect our thinking and acting about the present Latin American situation? What is the church's task? What is the Christian's responsibility? In order to find our way with these questions let us for a while concentrate our attention on the way in which God acts in our world.

God at Work in the World

As Christians we know that God *has acted* in the past, reaching his decisive work in the person of Jesus Christ; that he *will act* in the last day of this world, openly revealing and fulfilling in a final way his work in Jesus Christ; and that now in the meantime, between the decisive act in Jesus Christ and its final disclosure, he *is working*. In the limits of this chapter we have to content ourselves with recalling a few aspects of this threefold conviction.

God's decisive act in Jesus Christ is the one toward which he had been working since the beginning of sinful human history. The center of this act is the cross on which Jesus Christ died after a life of perfect humility and obedience, identifying himself with all men, taking upon himself their wickedness, not seeking retaliation nor nourishing a grievance. Thus in Jesus' death, human wickedness, the power of evil, is destroyed. On the cross "he disarmed the principalities and powers." (Col. 2:15) His is a complete victory because through his full identification with men, his death has vicarious value for all of them. "God was in Christ reconciling the world to himself." (2 Cor. 5:19)

Jesus' identification with man in his death is also effective in his resurrection: "I have been crucified with Christ; it is no longer I who live, but Christ who lives in me." (Gal. 2:20) The fact of our participation in the victory over death, the final enemy, indicates that something unique and of a decisive nature has taken place, something that has started a definitive new era, something that has been done once for all and needs no repetition: "If anyone is in Christ, he is a new creation; the old has passed away, behold, the new has come." (2 Cor. 5:17)

This does not mean, however, final fulfillment or consummation. The old life of the world still goes on. We know this only too well. That is why, as Christians, we also know that there is still future work to be done: the total disclosure of God's decisive action in Jesus Christ.

We must be satisfied with knowing that the final consummation will be entirely the work of God and not the result of the action of the state, nor of the self-discipline of the conscience, nor of the process of nature. If all the corrupted powers have been defeated on the cross, the final victory can only be the Parousia—the coming in glory—of him who once was crucified.

God's Present Work

But what is God doing meanwhile, in the period stretching from the Resurrection to the Parousia, in our time? This period is called the time of God's patience or forbearance because "the Lord is not slow about his promise, . . . but is forbearing toward you, not wishing that any should perish, but that all should reach repentance." (2 Pet. 3:9) We are, then, living in the time when God is making known to everyone the Good News in Jesus Christ, which brings about repentance, faith, and knowledge of the truth. And God is doing this because his love embraces the whole creation.

This period is also called the time of the church because all those who repent, believe, and know the truth—who discover and accept the wonderful identification of Christ with them—constitute the new people of God called the church. They are all one because they are all identified with Christ. In between the Resurrection and the Parousia God is building up his one church.

The church is sent to preach, to proclaim the name of him in whom men may believe. "As the Father has sent me, even so I send you." (John 20:21) "Go into all the world and preach the gospel to the whole creation." (Mark 16:15) "Make disciples of all nations." (Matt. 28:19) The period from the Resurrection to the Parousia may also be called the time of the mission of the church.

This does not mean that God is not also acting outside the church, independently of it. All the natural and sociological powers of the world are, since the cross, well in his hands. He not only allows them to subsist, on account of his forbearance, but he even uses them for the very work he is at present accomplishing.

God's sovereignty over natural and political powers reminds us that the liberation accomplished by Christ is of cosmic dimensions. He did not come just to save individuals but to redeem the whole world: "for in him all the fullness of God was pleased to dwell, and through him to reconcile to himself all things, whether on earth or in heaven. . . ." (Col. 1:19, 20) This cosmic redemption has been decisively accomplished on Golgotha and will be fulfilled with the disclosure of the Last Day but, for the same reason that God is acting at present, this cosmic redemption is also taking place now.

It follows that human works and institutions are capable of redemption; they can be brought within the Christian dispensation and be directed not merely by natural ethics but by the ethics of the gospel. The church must, therefore, pronounce the name of Jesus Christ not only with its implications for individuals but also with its meaning for all corporate beings. What have been called "the intellectual gospel" and "the social gospel" are constituent elements of the task of the church.

Two difficulties of different kinds stand on this path of obedience. The first one lies in the fact that the church, though heavenly, is embodied in human existence, that is to say, as a sociological phenomenon. Her message, therefore, has to be confirmed by her life as a sociological reality. When testifying to the corporate implications of the cross, she must be a living demonstration of what corporateness is. She cannot resignedly accept the divisions that cultural and political powers have brought and are trying to bring into her existence. She must remember the prayer of her Lord "that they may all be one . . . so that the world may believe." (John 17:21) While accomplishing her task in the world, the church has to strive to be the Church.

The other difficulty arises from the fact that it is not easy to know with accuracy when a corporate reality is coming into being, or growing, or in full maturity, or on the decline, or dying, or dead. Consequently, it is hard to know when it has to be baptized, or nourished, or respected, or criticized, or mourned over, or buried. This difficulty requires constant alertness for discerning the signs of the times. All static positions with regard to the structures of our world jeopardize the mission of the church. Our prayer must be that the love of all Christians "may abound more and more, with knowledge and all discernment, so that [they] may approve what is excellent and may be pure and blameless for the day of Christ." (Phil. 1:9, 10)

A few Biblical passages indicate that this "day of Christ" depends, as it were, on the task of the church: "This gospel of the kingdom will be preached throughout the whole world as a testimony to all nations; and then the end will come." (Matt. 24:14) "Repent . . . and turn again . . . that he may send the Christ." (Acts 3:19, 20; see also 2 Pet. 3:11, 12) Here is powerful incentive to mission for all those who, having tasted the kindness of God, long for the day when he will be everything to everyone.

The Task of the Church in Latin America Today

By way of linking up the two preceding sections on the Latin American situation today and on the way God acts in history, I wish to offer some general considerations about the church's task in Latin America today.

To start with, can we say that the church has had a genuine influence on the life of the Latin American countries? It seems hard to do so. The church of Jesus Christ has been represented during more than four and a half centuries. During the three centuries of the colonial period, the Roman Catholic Church completely dominated the situation and since independence, in spite of many anti-clerical manifestations, it has managed to go on occupying a pre-eminent place. But "the cowl does not make the monk." The prevalence of a purely nominal Roman Catholicism, denounced even by members of the hierarchy, indicates that actually Latin America has not been deeply Christianized. How could a region that has had a history of so much social injustice be said to have been molded by the gospel?

During the last hundred years the church of Jesus Christ has also been represented in Latin America by Protestant churches. Some of them came into existence through European immigration. Others have been the result of evangelistic work, proceeding often from North America, undertaken on the correct assumption that Latin America is a "mission land." These churches have been growing in an amazing way and at present their membership is estimated to be between five and six millions. But it would be a great exaggeration to say that they have deeply influenced the life of the Latin American countries. Certainly they have transformed hundreds of thousands of individual lives, and many of their members have been able, through moral behavior and by word of mouth, to bring into the Christian dispensation their immediate social setting, such as the family, the office, and the workshop. But the witness of the churches, as such, has rarely made any impact on the political and cultural life of the whole country.

Several reasons explain this. The Protestant churches have met great opposition and they have been persecuted. They have usually been considered foreign and allowed to exist on condition that they would remain on the fringes of national life. They have, until now, been a small minority not deeply convinced about the possibility of becoming influential in civil life. Due to the kind of Christian perversion they were facing, they have had to insist, since the beginning, on the personal character of Christian faith. Being dragged along by this emphasis, they have not been able to avoid irresponsible individualism in which there is great concern for the believer's own blessedness and carelessness for the life of the world. Therefore, when we say that the church has had little genuine influence on the life of the Latin American countries, we are referring not only to the Roman Catholic Church—whose responsibility is greater on account of its longer existence and its privileged position— but also to the Protestant churches.

With this in mind, let us see what should be the present task of the church as it seeks to take part in God's work in Latin America. Three main things may be said about this task, if we are answering the question as members of Protestant churches.

A Vital Biblical Base

First, the churches of Latin America must strive to have their faith and message firmly rooted in what God has done in a decisive manner in Jesus Christ. True, the Protestant churches have always emphasized the utmost importance of the Holy Scriptures, which contain the full account of God's work in Jesus Christ. In fact, it is by the introduction of the Bible that the Evangelical faith has entered Latin America. Many stories could be told about the wonderful way in which the holy book, through its mere distribution, has won lives to Jesus Christ. The Bible is so much in the hands and in the mouths of Evangelical Christians that it is usually considered, in other circles, as a Protestant book.

But does this mean that the faith and message of the Protestant churches are always entirely Biblical? No. Sometimes the gospel is presented as a moral doctrine or a sort of philosophy about the nature of God, instead of as what

35

God has done in Jesus Christ; at other times one of the many ways in which the Bible proclaims the gospel is singled out as its only true interpretation.

It is not too strong to say that in Latin American countries even the Protestant churches are in need of a new discovery of the Bible. They need Biblical scholars who, knowing that they are not God's word-protectors but that the Word of God will protect them, will not be afraid of examining thoroughly the written text in order to discover more fully God's infinite richness. Only through renewed amazement before the great acts of God will the Christian faith be a living one and the Christian message relevant to the listeners' situation. We may add that only with such a thorough Biblical faith and message will the Protestant churches challenge the Roman Catholic Church to go back to the Bible. We must hope for a growing Biblical concern in the Roman church, knowing that if both Roman Catholic and Evangelical Christians root themselves in what God has done in Jesus Christ, God's present work in the world will be all the more powerful and fruitful.

Faith Confirmed

In the second place, the churches of Latin America should endeavor to confirm their faith and preaching not only through the personal behavior of their members but also through their lives as reconciled communities. The transformation of individual lives and an impact on the working class rank among the greatest achievements of the Latin American Protestant churches. Ceasing to be a drunkard, no longer squandering one's wages, being able to send one's children to school, raising one's standard of life—such personal changes provoke questions. The explanation is simple: "I have become an Evangelical Christian; I have discovered that Jesus Christ cleanses me of all my sins; come to my church with me and learn for yourself."

Soon, however, the newcomer will discover that he is not going just to an Evangelical Church but to a Baptist, Methodist, Lutheran, Plymouth Brethren, Pentecostal, Episcopal, Neo-Apostolic, Disciples of Christ, Nazarene, Adventist, Presbyterian, or still another church. Often, depending on the church he is visiting, he will hear that this or that other Evangelical church is heretical, or formalist, or too much like the Roman church, or modernist, or fundamentalist. The tone of the remark will hardly allow him to take it as a positive description. Moreover, he will very often be involved in internal dissensions and may have to decide which of the divided groups he should follow.

There is an urgent need, therefore, to grasp the fact that this evil power of divisiveness also has been defeated on the cross and that the reconciliation achieved by Jesus Christ can only result in one church, which in its missionary task must manifest its oneness both within each congregation and among all congregations corporately. The Latin American churches need to understand that the ecumenical movement is an integral part of the church's mission and that all the discussions about denominational loyalty and church re-union are only right if they are carried on in a missionary perspective. They should also realize that the co-operation achieved in federations or councils of churches is legitimate only as a means and never as a goal. If co-operation is not made an end in itself, the Protestant churches will be ready to be led into new and unforeseen situations in which their witness will be strengthened by a fuller manifestation of Christian unity.

This readiness does not mean passivity but availability, and this entails all kinds of efforts to get rid of hindrances accumulated by the stream of history. The Latin American churches need experts on church history, on the historical development of doctrinal formulation, on the circumstantial reasons for such or such form of the church's order and worship—experts who will interpret the past in order to help the churches accomplish their present task.

There is need for serious theological work, not carried on in isolated studies, but going hand in hand with a committed witness. Only when fully engaged in theological work and ecumenical missionary work will Protestants be entitled to hope for the establishment of true conversations with those Roman Catholics who are deeply concerned with bringing the gospel of Jesus Christ to pagan Latin America. And when these much more difficult manifestations of Christian unity take place, the church of Jesus Christ will show, in the most powerful way, that reconciliation in Jesus Christ is not an idle expression.

Culture, Politics, and the Gospel

In the third place, the Latin American churches must learn to take seriously the implications of the cosmic redemption in Jesus Christ for the cultural and political powers of their continent. This situation offers great openings to Evangelical Christian influence. But to take advantage of them, the Protestant churches need wide, comprehensive vision. Until the present their vision has been limited, either by their particular European origins or by the unavoidably Anglo-Saxon imprint left by missionary work. They need members versed in literature, the arts, and philosophy, who are capable both of interpreting to their constituencies what is going on in the world of culture and of taking part, competently and effectively, in the development of culture. In the same manner, the Latin American churches are in great need of social and political experts who would interpret and influence the present social and political trends. Christian witness has great opportunities in the turbulence and upheaval of today; provided, on the one hand, that it is grounded in an understanding of what is happening and, on the other, that it springs, not out of fear—not even fear of communism, but out of the conviction that Jesus Christ has defeated all the powers of evil and that consequently all of those powers—even those of popular democracies—are capable of redemption.

The task confronting the church in Latin America is of huge proportions. In order to perform it, the Protestant churches need, as also does the Roman church, help from outside. But it is clear that this aid must now be specialized. Mere enthusiasm without some scholarly knowledge in one of the urgent fields of action will not be of great help. Specialized knowledge, enthusiasm, and adaptability, all are requirements for those who desire to take part in the thrilling missionary task in Latin America today—the task of witnessing to God's work in Jesus Christ, bringing about repentance and faith in him, showing what reconciliation is, striving to bring all kinds of corporate bodies within the Christian dispensation; in other words, performing God's present work.

EDMUND K.

SHERRILL

I have been in Brazil since 1953 and at present am serving as the Missionary Bishop of Central Brazil in the *Igreja Episcopal Brasileira,* counterpart of the Protestant Episcopal Church. The two other bishops with whom I serve are Brazilian.

While serving as an enlisted man in Europe during World War II, I came to a personal realization of the urgency of the church's world-wide mission. This conviction grew on soil prepared by boyhood experiences. My father, Bishop Henry Knox Sherrill, former Presiding Bishop of the Episcopal Church and a President of the World Council of Churches, was often host to churchmen from a wide range of nations. This paternal example of concern and involvement in the world church has been a continuing inspiration to me.

Interest in Latin America also dates back to war time. After the war ended, I attended a GI University set up in Biarritz, France. Somewhat to my disappointment the only course offered in history was on the Latin American area. Contrary to expectations, the course proved to be absolutely fascinating.

After the war I returned to Yale University where I was active in the Student Christian Movement. The influence of the SCM was decisive not only in sharpening my awareness of the world-wide church but also in laying the foundations of a continuing concern about the church's mission to the university. After graduation from the Episcopal Theological School, I served as assistant at Christ Church in Cambridge, Mass., where there were many opportunities for contact with Christian work in higher education. In Brazil, friendships formed through the SCM have been among the most stimulating I have known.

Although I now live in Rio de Janeiro, the first five years of my service in Brazil were spent as rector of a parish in São Paulo. This great city, a melting pot of people from all over the world, and the home of some of the most distinguished Christian leaders on the continent, afforded so many profound experiences that an undying love for the people of Brazil has been built in me and an unshakable faith in the capacity of Brazilian Christians for true witness.

40

CHAPTER TWO

THE RELIGIOUS SITUATION

by Edmund K. Sherrill

Not long ago the Foursquare Gospel came to São Paulo, Brazil. There was a good deal of publicity regarding the meetings, which were held in large tents strategically located in various parts of town. These tents were called *"Tendas da Cura Divina,"* "Tents of Divine Cure." The meetings included preaching, hymn singing, and prayers, but a major emphasis was on the cure of the sick, who came or were brought in large numbers. Some of the missionaries were very well prepared indeed and spoke fluently in Portuguese. Some seemed to rely more on enthusiasm and devotion. At any rate, the mission was a marked and rapid success, and there is now another established and growing religious group in Brazil. It is sad to relate, however, that relationships with established Christian churches are not good, and that this group is regarded by many as divisive, theologically unsound, and fanatical.

If you were to visit a certain, not unimportant Brazilian city you would find that the Roman Catholic churches in that place are served and operated by several priests from the United States. These men have been in charge of about one hundred small congregations for the past fifteen years. They are able and devoted missionaries and they have succeeded in significant measure in their work in spite of the lack of priests of Brazilian nationality in their area. There are several Protestant churches at work in the same place but Protestants and Roman Catholics maintain little contact

41

with one another. Like the Foursquare Gospel people, these men—both Protestant and Roman Catholic—are foreign missionaries, and their activities and attitudes are in some ways indicative of the religious situation in Brazil. For the fact is that foreign missions and missionaries have to a great extent determined the course and content of religious history throughout the area of Latin America, and that they continue to exercise a strong influence.

The missionary has two strong tendencies that are especially germane to the present inquiry: he is inclined to be intolerant, and he is intensely practical. In comparison with the priest, the educator, or the pastor per se, the missionary is after more tangible, measurable results, and proposes to adopt means to reach them. He seeks converts to build up his church, he seeks clearly defined issues to set before people for decision, he seeks to set his message off from what anybody else might be saying. At the same time he is continually forced in practice to make concessions because he cannot completely mold persons into the form that he would consider ideal. Following the model of the missionary, religious groups in Latin America are inclined to be intolerant and intensely practical.

Missionary Heritage

The Roman Catholic Church in this part of the world is still largely dominated by its experience as a colossal missionary enterprise. The identification of empire with church in both Spain and Portugal and in their possessions in the Americas, the mixture of secular and religious motives in both the conquistadors and the clerics, and the concessions made by the missionaries to indigenous religions in order to sweep converts into the fold have been described by many able writers.

The point here is merely that the Roman Catholic today lives very close to this enormous effort. There is the same fanatical and intolerant spirit, the same eye for the main chance, the same use of political, economic, and even military power where possible, the same hope that through some stunning use of power or showmanship great forward strides can be taken. Furthermore, certain aspects of the present situation encourage the continuation of this militancy. "The masses have slipped away; let us go after them with the same old methods." "The Protestants and the Communists are abroad in the land; forward against the foe!" In the main the Roman Catholic Church has not come to terms with the fact that things are now fundamentally different, and that God requires, and men need, a different spirit.

Most Protestant churches at work in Latin America are very definitely missionary organizations, too. They are the result of about one hundred years of serious effort principally on the part of North Americans. Many of them have come a long way against the tide of prejudice, ignorance, slander, and outright oppression that was raised up against them. Thus their mentality and their methods have been formed by this costly missionary effort, and certain factors that continue into the present with almost undiminished force encourage the continuation of the same way of life. The most important, of course, is that the Roman church is still there and shows little inclination to modify its fundamental attitudes. Also, in spite of great strides forward, Protestantism has not yet established its place in the sun and is still hungry for the power to influence events and protect itself from harm. Finally, the vast mission field still beckons—millions of persons sunk in ignorance and superstition, still wait to hear the saving word of Evangelical Christianity. All of this means a missionary mentality with its virtues and its flaws: it means a militant denominational definition against the Roman church and against other Protestant competitors; it means an obsession with the church, without a doctrine of the church; an emphasis on mission without a profound theology of mission.

The traditional churches face a turbulent society that, like all others, is a long way from being dominated for Christ. A variety of non-Christian religions are extremely powerful. Spiritualism appears in a variety of forms, from esoteric cults that appeal to more intellectual types, to the Umbanda and Macumba varieties, which use African and indigenous motifs and rituals as a means of bringing benefits to the worshipers. It is difficult also to make a clear distinction between Christian and non-Christian movements, and opinions vary greatly as to where the line should be drawn. The Christian community shades off through a variety of sects, mostly of North American origin, some of which are far, far away from orthodoxy in any recognizable form. Yet even the strangest of the spiritualist religions incorporate some Christian influence in doctrine, Scripture, or sacrament.

All this goes on against a background of basic materialism. Many are consciously materialist and regard any religion, especially the traditional one, as futile and irrelevant. Huge numbers are unconsciously in a worse state than this might suggest in that they adopt a given religious position in order to obtain certain material advantages and judge the various possibilities by that measure. The infiltration of these attitudes into the traditional churches is all too evident. In some cases such attitudes manifest themselves in a readiness to accept a permanent dependence upon funds from abroad or from the state and to pretend to a vitality and to a position that in fact do not exist. In some, they appear in vainglorious ambitions of both a personal and collective nature. All the churches run the terrible risk of worldliness.

The Theological Task

If this is in fact the religious situation, then certain things appear imperative to the present writer. In the first place, there is a tremendous intellectual task to be performed by the churches of Christ separately and together. Theological seminaries need to be greatly strengthened, not only to provide a more adequate education for ministers but also to serve as centers for prayer and profound reflection for the whole Christian community. There is a growing and significant number of able laymen who would have an important contribution to make if they were to become involved more deeply in the theological task.

There are various aspects to the task. The reading public is constantly growing everywhere on the continent, whereas the quality and quantity of Christian literature remain relatively low. The churches need to bring the social sciences to bear more effectively on the planning and execution of their mission. The Evangelical churches, unfortunately, tend to confine themselves to certain groups or classes in the general population, even though they have not consciously tried to do this. In the fields of education and social service the Christian enterprise cries out for modernization, better quality, and a more effective tie with the gospel itself.

This means that Latin America requires the very best that each denomination has to offer. This best should come to the continent, not so much through leaders imported from abroad (this has been too long a pattern for both Roman and Evangelical Christians), but through offering to Latin American leaders the most stimulating and educating experiences available in the Christian world. Moreover, a theological deepening must be an ecumenical experience. The ignorance that obtains among us concerning other denominations requires elimination before the theological task before us can be fruitfully undertaken. Furthermore, we ourselves, with our divisions and suspicions, our ignorance and intolerance, *are* a fundamental part of the theological task.

A special aspect here is once again the missionary heritage of Latin American Christianity. The influence of North America in the Evangelical churches has been sufficiently noted. The Roman Catholic Church also has historically been directed from abroad, openly in the colonial period, and today, although the hierarchy is national, there are too few vocations for the priesthood among the people of the land, with the result that strong contingents of foreign priests are on the job. There is a danger here that the Latin American churches be constantly trying to live up to someone else's ideal for them, whereas the real need is that they be strong in their own lands and among their own peoples, free, and in living contact with the rest of the Christian world. In no case is this more devoutly to be desired than in the traditional Roman Catholic Church. One says this not so much in benefit of the church as in the interest of the people of Latin America. No one is going to abolish the Roman church in the Americas, and Roman Catholics must see that the Protestant movement cannot now be eliminated or repressed in these lands. The continent needs the best that both the Roman church and Protestantism have to give.

No one is especially qualified to see the pair of glasses he himself is wearing. The Roman Catholic Church is undeniably imperialistic. That the Protestant movement in Latin America also has its imperialistic aspect is similarly true. Foreign missionaries may try with all sincerity to be only missionaries of Christ's empire, which is not of this world and which seeks no worldly power or influence. They are also, however, representatives of a complex agglomeration of political, cultural, and economic factors that deeply influence everything they do. Therefore they are not qualified to perform the theological task, to provide the profound interpretation of Christ's will for his church in Latin America that the times require. At the same time, Latin Americans alone cannot do the task, but need vital contact with Christian thought and Christian persons from all the world. This may occur through the international hierarchical structures of the Roman churches, or through the Protestant system of relations with mission boards and world denominational alliances. The important thing is that imperialism should end.

Worship and Mission

In the Christian life, reflection, meditation, and corporate prayer move together. The mission of the Body of Christ cannot be separated from that worship which binds believers sacramentally and mystically to the Lord and to one another in him. General statements are often dangerous, but let us run that risk. Christian worship in Latin America is the weakest aspect in the whole picture. While the liturgical movement may have brought renovation and renewal in some Roman Catholic circles elsewhere, its effects are not yet noticeable in Latin America. The worship experience offered is just about the opposite of the ideal. Besides what many would consider superstitions and pagan admixtures in the cult, one notes other weaknesses, perhaps even more serious. There is almost no understanding of ritual or participation in it on the part of the people. Each one worships as an individual seeking his own benefits. Community is not created by such worship. There are so many ugly and tawdry churches, so many rushed, mechanical, impersonal ceremonies, so much that passes for worship which is the opposite of a deep, personal, corporate experience of God's presence, that one wonders why so many continue to seek to answer their needs in this way. Roman believers in Latin America are not receiving what that church states it offers to its people in the way of worship. Liturgical reform has been attempted here and there, and some bishops have even tried to put a stop to some popular festivals and practices that cannot be squared with the Christian faith. But this is not enough. The whole situation cries out for a real reformation and some real education in liturgy and worship.

The Evangelical churches fail more evidently in this area than in any other. There are two sorts of error in the picture. Some enthusiastic sects compete with the Roman church in noisy spectacle, sentimentality, emotionalism, the search for

47

and the staging of miracle, and the promise of material benefit. Numerical and financial successes do not hide the fact
that this is not Christian worship. On the other hand, the
more established Evangelical churches present a picture of
liturgical poverty. The church tends to be an auditorium
gathered to hear a preacher read, pray, and deliver a message. While there is often strong participation in the singing,
the hymns are mostly uninspired translations of uninspired
English originals set to trivial or sentimental music. There
are too many ugly and tasteless churches, there is too much
emphasis on the person of the minister and his weekly speech,
too much imported material of inferior quality for this to
pass as anything but substandard Christian worship.

The peoples who live in Latin America have tremendous
cultural vitality, which expresses itself in music and dancing,
the use of color, the sense of drama, the new movements in
literature and in all the arts, the striking architecture—things
that have brought this part of the world to everyone's attention. With rare exceptions, however, the Christian churches,
both Roman and Evangelical, though for different reasons,
have not only failed to share creatively in this culture but
have really formed an atmosphere that suffocates and de-
stroys cultural expression. Freedom of worship must come
to mean the freedom not only to express ideas in words, but
also to celebrate and commemorate the mighty acts of God,
to sing the praise of the Divine Redeemer, to offer up the
world to God in forms of worship that are a living expression
of the faith and being of the worshipers themselves.

Perhaps it seems that hard words have been said about
missionaries, and foreign missionaries in particular. The present writer is a foreign missionary. Surely there is no grander
word in the Christian vocabulary than "missionary." It is a
pity to restrict it to the effort to build up church membership.
The mission of the church is discovered and expressed in

worship, in reflection, in responsibility for society, in cultural forms. All who are in Christ are missionaries, sent out into the world by their Lord. For that matter, in this world we are all in some sense foreigners, or as the Epistle to the Hebrews says, "strangers and exiles on the earth." But just the same it is of primary importance to recognize the limitations of foreign missionary efforts and to look anxiously for the day when the Christian churches of Latin America will bring into the world mission of the whole church all the richness of their own understanding and creativity.

Missionaries are peculiar people. They feel that they are sent by God himself in order to carry out his purpose in the world, and there is no joy equal to this joy in the knowledge and service of God. Sometimes it is hard to recognize that God has called others, some of them to greater honor and responsibility, some of them persons with whom it is difficult to agree. For the churches it is hard to co-operate in a practical and living way with God's power at work in another group. Christ's will in Latin America will not be done by any one church all by itself, not even by the traditional Roman Catholic faith, although the error of excluding that church from his sway is just as serious as its own pretensions to absoluteness. His will will not be done by foreign missionaries or by international hierarchies, committees, or boards of foreign missions either, although surely it is legitimate to hope that through these means the Christian world may live in constant and fruitful relationship with their brethren in this part of the earth. God's call in Latin America is addressed to Latin Americans. He will give to those whom he calls the power to think through, in faith and humility, the full meaning of the mission entrusted to them, and to live that mission in such a way that it becomes a living word of testimony to his power and glory.

GONZALO

BÁEZ-CAMARGO

A third generation Methodist, I was born in 1899 in Mexico's southern city of Oaxaca, the son of a school teacher. After my early education I went to the Mexican Methodist Institute in Puebla. At fifteen, I joined the revolutionary forces under Venustiano Carranza. Within a year's time I was seriously wounded in action and won a promotion, but decided to go back to school.

After graduation from Union Evangelical Seminary in 1921, I was taken seriously ill. A prompt and almost miraculous recovery, after the doctors had lost hope, gave me a deep sense of vocation. Having faced death a second time and received life again, I felt that God was preserving me for some special service.

After three years of pastoral work I entered the educational field as vice-president of my alma mater in Puebla. But in 1929 the recently formed National Evangelical Council of Mexico called me to serve as Executive and Secretary of Christian Education. Two years later I was asked to take on the additional responsibility of managing the Union Publishing House, a concern supported by several missionary organizations.

Writing has become for me an important avenue of witness in the world. A book of poetry, published while I was a theological student, was my first venture in print. Several books have followed. In 1930 I became a staff contributor to *Excelsior,* a leading newspaper in Mexico City. I am still writing for this paper. I also write for the magazine *Tiempo* and serve as correspondent in Mexico for *The Christian Century.*

I have served as a vice-president of the International Missionary Council and as a member of the Provisional Committee of the World Council of Churches. I am now a member of the Board of Managers of the World Council of Christian Education and Sunday School Association. From 1946 to 1960 I worked as Literature Secretary for the Committee on Cooperation in Latin America. I am now a translator for the American Bible Society and am teaching at Union Evangelical Seminary. I came to know students in the United States as a visiting professor both in Union Theological Seminary, New York and in Garret Biblical Institute, Evanston, Ill.

| CHAPTER THREE | QUESTIONS OF RACE AND PREJUDICE |
| | by Gonzalo Báez-Camargo |

In June, 1960, the decennial census of the population of Mexico was taken. As on previous occasions, no inquiry was made about race. This fact is in itself significant of Mexico's official attitude: racial differences are not acknowledged.

It is not easy, therefore, to give accurate statements about the country's present racial composition. Anthropological studies do, of course, provide some information. According to the more authoritative estimates, about 70 per cent of the population are mestizos or in various degrees mixed (mainly Spanish and Indian). Some 15 per cent are Indians, 11 per cent native or foreign-born persons of full European stock, and perhaps 4 per cent mulattoes, plus a negligible number of full Negro natives and aliens.

Generally speaking, there is no racial problem in Mexico. There is concern over the acute differences in cultural level and economic status that do exist between groups, but I find no sharp race consciousness except for a certain amount of pride in Indian and Spanish ancestry. The racial situation in Mexico does not, then, present the acute and bitter issues that may be seen elsewhere.

Two main factors were effective in creating this situation. The first was the nondiscriminatory attitude of the Spanish conquerors and original settlers of Mexico. The second was the nature and program of the revolution under whose inspiration the country is now moving forward, especially in its policy with regard to the Indian.

The Indian in Colonial Mexico

On the whole the Spaniards—and the same was true of the Portuguese in Brazil—did not mind taking Indian women as mistresses and sometimes legally as wives. When Cortes, after the Conquest, brought his Spanish wife from abroad to be with him, he gave his Indian mistress, Malintzi, in marriage to one of his captains. Later, when on a limited scale Negro slaves were imported from Africa, the Spaniards, similarly, intermarried with Negroes. In addition, there was considerable Indian-Negro intermarriage. The present population of Mexico has arisen through a complex intermixing of these three groups.

Of course, this fact does not mean that the early Spaniard dealt with these other races on grounds of equality. He mixed more with the Indian than with the Negro. And it was to a large extent the lack of Spanish women during the Conquest and their scarcity afterwards that led to mixed unions. These were mostly unions of Spanish men to Indian women, seldom the reverse. In many instances the Indian women were simply taken by force, but the fact that there was mixture one way or the other discouraged strict discrimination or segregation on racial grounds.

On the other hand, the Spanish system was based on the assumption that the Indian was actually an inferior. Even at its best, it treated the Indian as a minor who would never grow up and become self-sufficient. The Indians were mistreated, despoiled, and forced into servitude.

Great Spanish theologians, such as Vitoria and Suarez, and devoted missionaries, such as Las Casas, undertook the defense of the Indians against theoretical or practical denials of their equal rights as human persons. But in spite of that vigorous defense, the aborigines were kept under an iron yoke, either as perpetual minors or as actual serfs. After the first educational zeal of the early apostolic missionaries, the education of the Indians practically ceased. The highest positions in church and government were barred to them. For over two centuries even the common ranks of the priesthood were out of bounds for them.

This assumed superiority of the Spaniards over the natives was not, however, based strictly on racial considerations. It was more in the nature of a distinction between people born in Spain and the *naturales de la tierra*—the natives of the land. For as the number of people of mixed race, and of persons of pure Spanish blood but born in Mexico, increased, even the latter—called *criollos* (creoles)—were thrown back into a second-class category. They also were denied access to the highest positions in state and church, although they had managed to become, mainly by inheritance, owners of land, and were the best educated people in the country.

Ultimately, then, it was a matter of place of birth rather than race—it was Europeans versus Americans. High public officials, bishops, provincial authorities of religious orders, and other top leaders of the colony had to be people born in and coming straight from the Old Country.

As to the rest of the population, some racial considerations were nevertheless present. Colonial society was sharply divided into several strata. On the very top were Spaniards or "whites" born in Spain, a hand-picked minority who ruled church and state. Second to them were the *criollos,* the Spaniards born in Mexico. Then came the vast mass of people of mixed blood, classified in several groups, called castes, scaled according to the nature and degree of their mixture —Indian-Spanish, Negro-Spanish, Indian-Negro, Spanish-Mestizo, Spanish-Mulatto, Indian-Mulatto, etc. Then, at the bottom of all, was the Indian. But still, the economic and cultural level of the castes and of the Indians having been so low—in many cases subhuman—it is difficult to determine to what extent the discrimination they suffered was due to that reason or really to race as such.

Full Integration of Mexican Indians

With the coming of independence, this structure of colonial society soon began to give way. Creoles and educated mestizos—among them the lower echelons of the priesthood—led in the fight against European-held power. One of the first actions of the insurgents in 1810, when they sent out the call to insurrection, was to abolish slavery. In 1821, when Mexico at last became independent, all Mexicans were made equal before the law. Although wide social differences based on wealth and education continued, the way was now open for all Mexicans, regardless of race, place of birth, or social station, to move forward and upward in society by getting an education or acquiring wealth.

The whole range of Mexican life was thrown open to all, including the Indians—government, industry, art, science, agriculture, and the church. A full Indian, Benito Juarez, became the country's greatest president. At least two of the most loved and influential teachers and writers were also Indians: Altamirano and Ramirez. The vast majority of the Indians, nevertheless, and of the mestizos remained in a backward condition—but not because of any racial discrimination. Programs of economic progress and education were simply moving very slowly, and they spent themselves on their way down, so that they did not reach the lowest social levels.

Reaching these groups has been the work of the revolution that started in 1910 and came to a climax when its ideals and program became the law of the country and were embodied in the new Constitution of 1917. With the distribution of lands to the Indian and considerable emphasis on his education, he has received a new status and a new sense of worth as a human being. Whatever trace remained of the notion that he is born inferior has now been completely wiped away.

The creole and the mestizo have acquired a fresh appreciation of the values in pre-Hispanic Indian civilizations, thus paving the road for a vigorous cultural renewal. Also, with the advance in education, industrialization, and communications, which in turn brings an increase in mixed marriages, the Indian is being more and more absorbed into the general stream of national life.

The case of the Indian well illustrates the point that, in Mexico, whenever any attitude of prejudice against certain groups does exist, it is based mostly on social, economic, and national considerations, and is not specifically a matter of racial discrimination. All these kinds of prejudice are, of course, wrong for Christians. But race prejudice obviously is the worst of all prejudices because it holds against a human being something about which he can do nothing, even if he actually wishes to. By education and hard work, he can raise himself from a low social and economic level. By naturalization and cultural integration he can make differences in nationality disappear, at least for his children. Racial prejudice, on the other hand, forever imprisons a person in an iron-clad bracket. It imprisons his offspring equally.

Chinese and Jewish Minorities

Turning from the Indian to other ethnic minorities, it is possible to detect in Mexico a certain amount of prejudice and antipathy toward Chinese and Jews. Since so many of them have become Mexican citizens and since the census does not record ethnic groupings, no reliable figures are available as to their present numbers. The immigration laws in general are very strict regarding admission of aliens other than Latin Americans. This is particularly true in the case of Asians, but since World War II it has become true for Europeans as well. These limitations, however, are not grounded on race but on nationality, and are inspired by economic and demographic considerations only.

The Chinese, though still a minority group, are especially numerous along the Pacific coast, but they also have settled to some extent throughout Mexico. The frugality of the Chinese, including the fact that they work for lower wages than the average Mexican laborer, has created some economic tension in areas where Chinese are present in large numbers. A common prejudice entertained by Mexicans is that the Chinese really are an inferior breed, and that intermarriage with them will bring about a degeneration of the human stock. But this prejudice is largely a theoretical one. In actual practice, Chinese and Mexicans intermarry easily, and after one or two generations of such intermarriage the children become fully integrated.

As in practically every other country, the Jews in Mexico constitute an active and enterprising minority. With their well-known ability in business, most of them, even when starting from "scratch," readily acquire a living standard quite above the average. They soon become employers of Mexican labor. They tend to be a self-contained community, very seldom marrying non-Jews. The majority, however, soon take out their citizenship papers. But this fact, even when added to the generous Jewish support of schools, clinics, and other benevolences for the general good, does not always outweigh other factors, which are then made the basis for suspicion and anti-Semitic prejudice on the part of many people.

Here again it must be pointed out that this feeling arises from social, cultural, and economic, rather than strictly racial, considerations. And even this feeling has tended to subside as a result of effective public relations by Jewish organizations and by the State of Israel. These organizations have enlisted an increasing number of non-Jewish Mexicans who stand out in journalism, education, art, science, public office, and other influential fields of national life as friends and advocates of the Jewish people.

Feelings Against the U.S.A.

Some latent anti-U.S. feelings exist. They go back to unfortunate conflicts between the two countries and have been nurtured by incidents, resented by Mexicans, between the United States and other Latin American countries.

The fact that Mexico lost to the United States first Texas, then other extensive areas, adding up to more than half of its territory, during the war of 1847, has not altogether been forgotten by Mexicans.

Anti-U.S. feelings have been aroused also by more recent incidents. The Mexican Revolution was bitterly attacked and slandered by powerful financial interests in the United States. Then there was the landing of the United States Marines in Veracruz in 1914, and the Pershing expedition into northern Mexico in 1916. Mexico has felt as a wound in its own flesh and bone the taking of Panama under Theodore Roosevelt, the Platt Amendment on Cuba, the United States armed interventions in Santo Domingo and Nicaragua, and the fact that two of the worst dictators in Latin America—Trujillo and Somoza—were sorry left-overs of the American occupation in their countries.

A source of deep resentment among liberals and other progressive—but non-Communist!—groups in Latin America, has been the unfortunate tendency of United States foreign policy to pay little attention to democratic movements for social justice in Latin America and, at the same time, to extend goodwill and support to despots who represent themselves as bulwarks against communism. Why, such persons ask, should the United States, a pioneer of democracy, look with disfavor on young democracies in other countries? Is it that the United States stands for freedom, human rights, and democracy for its own people, but not for other peoples?

Many of these liberals, for instance, do not like Fidel Castro's policies in Cuba, but they keep asking why United

States opinion on the whole kept quiet when the Batista dictatorship was strangling Cuba in its bloody grip. They believe that Castro's downfall, since he sold out Cuba to the Soviet block, is highly desirable, but they resent deeply any United States government agency's attempt to set up and control an anti-Castro coup or invasion. They did not approve the murder of Somoza in Nicaragua, but they could not understand why President Eisenhower anxiously rushed a doctor to the despot's deathbed or why the President mourned him afterwards as a "dear friend" of the United States. And it is very hard for them to overlook the fact that it is mainly the support of the United States that keeps Hitler's and Mussolini's chum Francisco Franco in absolute power over Spain.

The spark of such anti-U.S. feeling was formerly fanned by the Roman Catholic Church as a defense against Protestant missionary work. Protestant missions, it was claimed, were only the spearhead of a "peaceful conquest" of Mexico and the rest of Latin America by the United States, a "Protestant power."

But with Roman Catholicism getting stronger in the United States, and Catholic missions now spreading in Latin America at a fast pace, the old story of "pacific conquest through missions" is proving a boomerang. So the Roman Catholics are changing their tune to a decidedly friendly one towards the "formerly Protestant" U.S.A. At present, the most active promoters of anti-U.S. feelings are the small but noisy minority of communists.

But again, to the extent to which it exists, feeling against the United States is more nationalistic than racial, and more often than not it takes the form of a general and abstract antipathy. Ordinarily, the individual North American is secretly admired and treated with spontaneous friendliness. It is the United States as a whole, especially its government's foreign policy and the activities of its big financial interests in Latin America, that is looked upon with suspicion and fear—such fear as any weak nation is likely to feel in the face of a powerful, energetic neighbor who is a not-always-tactful extrovert.

Super-patriotism can become a deeply entrenched prejudice. It is a subtle type of idolatry in which the collective ego is worshiped. The *we* may become a proud, aggressive weapon against the *they*. This is a danger that besets both weak and powerful nations. In Mexico, for instance, it takes the form of pride in "cultural traditions," considered to be highly "spiritual," and of contempt for the United States, to which a sheer materialistic outlook and utter lack of aesthetic interests are attributed. It is the sublimated revenge of a nation painfully conscious of its inferiority in material progress and technical skills.

The counterpart of this kind of nationalism is, of course, the assumption that progress and welfare must by all means require the wholesale adoption of the "American way of life" by every other country in the world. And this means not only in certain material conveniences and industrial techniques but also in a particular outlook on life and the world, in social structure and economic organization, in ways of thinking, and, above all, in "going along" with the United States in international policy and engagements. Modification of United States policy toward Latin America, and doing away, eventually, with all forms of racial segregation and discrimination in the United States, are imperative if United States influence and prestige are to be enhanced throughout the vast area to the south.

A Ministry of Understanding

God's purpose and action with regard to racial issues seems clearly revealed to us through the Holy Scriptures. All men have a common ancestry, a common Creator and a common Father, who is God—God of the whole universe,

Lord of all nations and peoples, partial to none. Jesus Christ died for all men, and God's eternal purpose is to unite all men in him. The Christian law of love is color-blind, universal, all-embracing. As stated by leading anthropologists, the findings of modern science clearly deny the existence of inferior or superior races, and thus are in accord with the essence of Christian teaching. In the light, therefore, of both science and the gospel, racial prejudice, discrimination, and segregation make no sense.

In their own life and work, Mexican Protestant churches entertain no racial prejudices or discrimination. The same may be said of the Roman Catholic Church. There exist, however, certain congregations for foreign residents that tend to lead a self-contained life, with very little or no communion with the Mexican churches. These foreign congregations—mainly English- and German-speaking—have, of course, a linguistic *raison d'être*. And they accept educated Mexicans who speak their language, an evidence that this kind of "voluntary segregation" is not ultimately grounded on strict racial considerations. They appear to the Mexicans, however, as a religious expression of the well-known tendency of foreigners in Mexico to stand aside as an aloof little island of fellow citizens in a strange country. This interpretation is reinforced by the fact that most of these foreign Christians, even when they are conversant in Spanish, do not usually seek fellowship with their Mexican brothers and sisters in Christ.

The existence of these foreign congregations, leading a more or less isolated life, fails to strengthen the witness of the Mexican churches in a situation already surcharged with the common prejudice that "Protestantism is an exotic, Anglo-Saxon religion." The common witness to the gospel by Evangelical Christianity, already weakened by self-asserting denominationalism, thus exposes itself to further blows. The tragedy of it all is intensified by the fact that it is already difficult for the Mexican churches to "raise a signal," to hold forth their witness in a land where they are overwhelmed by an often hostile non-Protestant majority.

The witness of Mexican Protestantism is indirectly but effectively hampered by the existence of racial discrimination and segregation in countries having a large Protestant majority, such as South Africa and the United States. This is particularly true in relation to the United States, from which most of our missionaries come and where, to make things still worse, there are zones where Mexicans themselves are subject to certain kinds of discrimination. Mexican Protestants are greatly shocked when they discover that many churches in whole areas of the United States compromise with social pressures and permit discrimination in their worship and fellowship.

Some press releases, while playing up any indication of nondiscrimination in the Roman Catholic Church, also play up practices in Protestant churches or statements from Protestant sources that seemingly support racial discrimination. Much less publicity, of course, is given to the notable progress in race relations that is taking place in the United States.

Here lies a challenge to the Protestant churches in Mexico —a challenge to make those positive advances better known here and to work incessantly through education, the press, and the pulpit toward a better understanding between two nations God has made close neighbors. Also, by what they are and do in their own country, Christians in the United States can strengthen the church's witness both there and here.

MAURICIO

LOPEZ

I got to know the gospel in Mendoza. A missionary couple of the Plymouth Brethren became interested in our family and they visited us frequently. The testimony of these people, their sympathy, and concern that we should accept the Word of God made a deep impression on me. With the death of the missionary, Luis Roberts, I realized that the peace and calm displayed by his wife in the most painful moments could only come from a sincere faith in God and in his grace. I then made my decision to receive the Lord's mercy and to follow Jesus Christ. I was nineteen years of age.

In the company and pastoral care of another missionary, James R. Taylor, in the life of prayer and reading of the Scriptures, in the communion with my brethren in the faith and in the testimony of the gospel, I began to take the church seriously as the body of Jesus Christ and to see the necessity of Christians being one in him. Thus the ecumenical movement appeared to me, from the very first, as one of the most remarkable works that the Spirit of God is accomplishing in our time.

I studied philosophy at the University of Cuyo. News began to reach me of the existence of a student movement in Buenos Aires linked with the World Student Christian Federation. I was able to profit somewhat from the life and inspiration of that group although it was more than six hundred miles away. In 1950, I took part in a camp, organized by the SCM in Las Flores, Uruguay. Since then I have felt a keen desire that God might use me in student work.

One afternoon in 1955 at a WSCF conference in Bolivia, Philippe Maury and Valdo Galland came to talk with me. To my surprise, they wished to propose my name to be Valdo's successor as Latin American Secretary of the WSCF.

In the period of time I requested before replying, I believed I sensed that the will of God was leading me to say yes. I trusted that he would supply what was lacking in me as to personal qualities, knowledge, and experience. I was appointed in Tutzing in August, 1956. It has been a great joy to be able to serve the church of Jesus Christ from the university outpost.

CHAPTER FOUR | # THE UNIVERSITY FRONTIER

by Mauricio Lopez

The Latin American tradition of higher learning reaches more than four centuries into the past. The first university to be established in the Spanish colonies was that of San Marcos in Peru. It was founded in 1538 and its work has continued uninterrupted since then. The University of Mexico rivals that of San Marcos in age, but it has suffered from certain periods when its life was disrupted. Scattered over the vast area of Latin America, eight centers of higher education were established before Harvard University opened its doors in 1636.

Changing Society, Changing University

In their historical development the Latin American universities have closely reflected their models, the teaching centers of Latin Europe. Three clearly defined movements have successively found expression in our universities: the Scholastic, the Positivist, and the Reform movements.

The Scholastic University was characteristic of the colonial period and was inspired by the Spanish models of Salamanca and Alcala. It possessed a unifying principle, the idea of God as the beginning and end of all human knowledge. Theology was the central and decisive discipline, with the full range of the sciences revolving around it. The Roman Catholic Church and the religious orders were largely responsible for teaching. In this situation the intellectual leadership that the universities developed tended to be composed mainly of members of the clergy. The university enjoyed autonomy in relation to the power of the government. Students took an active part in directing the life of the university. While students belonged normally to the privileged classes, it is also true that toward the end of the seventeenth century the sons of Indian chiefs were admitted to the university cloisters.

In the course of time, decay overtook the humanistic culture that had been transmitted through the university, leaving only dry and sterile formalism without that which is of basic importance, stimulation to free intellectual activity. The university became wholly impervious to the advances of experimental science. With the advent of political changes that brought independence from the colonial powers and gave rise to the new Latin American nations, the colonial university was bound to succumb to the new historical tides.

The Positivist university followed the Scholastic. With emancipation from colonial rule, the university threw off its colonial vestments. Inspired now by the model that the French Revolution produced, the universities of the new republics imposed upon education a purely utilitarian definition. They renounced any guiding philosophic principle in the name of ideological neutrality, and they concentrated mainly on the professional training of the ruling classes. The university became dispersed in professional schools of law, medicine, philosophy, etc., without any links between them. They were separate organisms under the auspices of the state; their gradual secularization would eventually mean the total eclipse of the theological disciplines that were characteristic of the colonial university. Attention was paid to the educational necessities of a bourgeois society—open, expansive, and conscious of its capacity to rule. Freedom of thought was always allowed and an atmosphere created that was favorable to the development of science and technological advancement.

This university began to decline after World War I. It was not prepared for a mass society, and it lived apart from the formative currents and forces in its own country. Nation and university moved in different spheres. In the Faculties of Law in Buenos Aires, all the details of the written law were taught but nothing was said about the meaning of justice in the midst of the particular social and economic developments through which the country was then passing.

The Reformist university had its birth pangs in a student rebellion against a university accused of being "conservative," "unilateral," "oligarchic," and "at the service of a pre-established order." The movement began with the student revolt in Cordoba, Argentina, and spread all over Latin America. The students called for changes in university life as well as in social and political conditions in their countries. In the university they were determined to democratize education by opening the university to all social classes as well as through optional attendance at classes, freedom of thought and teaching, the periodic character of the professorship, social services on behalf of the students, and the participation of students and graduates in the government of the university.

The Reformist movement reached the majority of countries, although the proposed changes were not applied in the same manner everywhere. Brazil's response to the Reformist demands was little more than lukewarm, while Bolivia tried to apply them with perhaps the greatest vigor, especially regarding the equality of students, graduates, and professors in directing the affairs of the university. This movement of reform reached the state universities and in a smaller measure the private colleges. Its influence was almost negligible in Roman Catholic universities. Outside the university the Reformist movement stimulated both social concern, expressed for instance in the Apra[1] movement in Peru, and political action evident in sharpened anti-colonial attitudes and belligerence toward all military dictatorships.

Perhaps the two most important innovations were the participation of the students in determining the direction of the university (already practiced in the medieval University of Bologna!), and the greater concern for the university's responsibility in society. Both these innovations were, however, weapons with a double edge. The new participation of the students contributed both to a greater consciousness among them of the nature of university life and to a greater dedication among professors to their teaching vocation. But student participation was considered an end in itself and sowed the seeds of lack of discipline, difficult to root out later. The impression exists today that student participation served only to make professional titles available with a minimum of effort through suppression of entrance examinations, an almost permanent absenteeism from classes, duplication of grades, and the expulsion of exacting examiners. The Positivist emphasis on the materialistic character of education was retained.

Everyone, of course, is aware of the particular social and political conditions of our countries that have made students the most effective champions of civil liberty and the decisive factor in the overthrow of totalitarian governments. The cases of Argentina, Colombia, Venezuela, Cuba, and the bloody repressions in Guatemala and Haiti, are examples that need no commentary. Equally certain, however, is the fact that student enthusiasm and lack of experience have formed an important weapon, cleverly utilized toward political and demagogic ends. Today the Reform has become a sacred myth that for its own good is in the process of being desecrated. *Universitas reformata reformanda est.*[2]

Quantity and Quality

Since World War II, three closely related phenomena may be observed. They are provoking a fresh awakening of the conscience of the university to the demands of its mission. The first of these is the extraordinary rhythm of the population growth and movement, considered today as one of the most explosive in the world. The population of Latin America has been making amazing increases in recent years, accompanied by a gradual movement from the country to the city. This has had a direct effect on the university atmosphere. At the University of Mexico, for instance, in 1929, the epoch in which the university won its autonomy, the student population was eight thousand. Now, thirty years later, it has increased more than seven times to the figure of sixty thousand.

It is evident that under these conditions the university cannot meet this extraordinary demand without the level of teaching being affected. Previously the university would complete the education of a select minority by providing professional specialization. Complete, I say, because the foundation was supplied by the public school and by an ample training received within the home. Today, as a rule, in a mass society the education of the student belongs wholly to the public educational system; the family contributes very little. The secondary school, however, has been unable to meet the needs of the population increase. In Costa Rica, for instance, in recent years secondary schools have had to be improvised right and left, and primary school teachers have had to teach in them.

In view of lack of preparation for higher education, there is a considerable university movement to ascertain the vocational capacities of candidates in an effort to distribute students in different schools as satisfactorily as possible. There is also the recourse of limiting by quotas the enrollment in the different university schools and departments. But this is only a half-solution to the problem. The students emigrate to other centers. It is said that there are about a thousand Nicaraguans in Mexico and as many Peruvians in Argentina. Such migration only accentuates the problem as well as creating another, that of those who do not return to their own country. Even when entrance is limited to those who fulfill the minimal conditions demanded, it is doubtful whether the university can satisfactorily fulfill its mission in the situation created by the intellectual and technical requirements of modern times.

Technological Demands

The second phenomenon refers to the demands of a society that is becoming increasingly diversified owing to its industrial development. In our universities we begin to see a serious preoccupation with meeting the needs of a society which, for its economic well-being, requires highly specialized professionals and technicians. Plans have been made to adapt the traditional structure of the universities to a revolutionary present such as exists in Latin America. We are still at the beginning, and there remains much to do before we can get rid of an organizational pattern that grew out of cultural ideas that have now been totally left behind.

It is now obvious that our modern society needs more than lawyers, doctors, accountants, and engineers. In Brazil more than 50 per cent of the students still continue under the influence of ancient customs of higher learning, and they overcrowd the courses in law and literature while the polytechnical and agricultural courses show unbelievably low enrollments.

It must be said that the university here faces a double problem: on the one hand, the demands of research and of technical development have led necessarily to the creation of research and teaching institutes outside the university. In these institutes an exclusively technico-scientific culture is being developed completely separate from the general culture. Yet any scientific culture that claims to be valid and useful for the social development of the nation must find its roots in this general culture. On the other hand the university, awake to the scientific needs of our time, faces the problem of how to introduce elements of general culture, including the humanities, at levels where teaching is of necessity already specialized.

One of the happiest attempts at solution of these difficulties has been the creation of the General Studies program at the University of Rio Piedras, in Puerto Rico. This program was later incorporated by the University of Costa Rica and is in the course of being adopted by the universities of Central America. Another solution is being tried in the Central University of Venezuela and in the Autonomous University of Mexico. In these cases general culture is considered not so much a body of knowledge as an attitude to be measured by the relations within the university itself and by the esthetic and cultural activities directed by the specialized institutions. This, of course, requires the organization of a communal university life. To achieve this end, university campus communities have recently been established all over the continent. The first was the University of Concepción in Chile; the most brilliant is that of Mexico; while the one in Buenos Aires is just beginning to acquire land and buildings.

National Identity and Destiny

The third phenomenon that unquestionably has repercussions in the university is an ever growing consciousness of the identity and destiny of the Latin American nations. There is a growing and more responsible consideration of national realities. With painful surprise the Latin American peoples have had to accept the hard fact of an underdeveloped economy resulting from a colonialist outlook. Fortunately, we have not given up in bitter resignation. We are struggling to develop our natural and cultural riches. In this exploration we not only are drawing upon traditional energies but also are turning to new methods that will awaken popular feeling and enthusiasm. In this sense Brasilia is a symbol of a nation that has rediscovered itself.

In what social philosophy these forces and ideas will take

form is still a question. The Latin American socio-political temper places itself between Frondizi's neoliberalism and Castro's Marxism. The recognition of two permanent ingredients of the Latin American character also offers clues: (1) an undeniable passion for liberty that is corrected at present by a concern for social justice, and (2) a receptiveness that at present is cautious about accepting without question all that is offered from outside.

This situation has its repercussions in the university. It may be observed in the ideological pluralism that reigns there. The state university, which has no racial problems and makes no religious discrimination, continues to be agnostic in its outlook without being anti-clerical. In the nineteenth century it was called the free-thinking university. Positivism survives certainly in Marxism, which makes continuing progress in intellectual circles and recruits the most active and vociferous among young students. Last year I had the opportunity of speaking with quite a number of Protestant students in Cuba. Some of them felt attracted by the economic solutions offered by communism, and at the same time they expressed severe criticism of their churches for the little or nothing done to live out the Christian presence with responsibility in that revolutionary situation.

Existentialism makes its influence felt, especially when dealing with the effort to ascribe identity to Latin America and to help the Latin American man find himself in relation to all his passions, his techniques, his natural surroundings, his cities, and his culture. The university is also the forum of a Roman Catholic Christian intelligentsia that, with the conceptual data of neo-Thomism, presents the principal problems of linking together faith and the diverse cultural attitudes of man. Roman Catholicism, as seen in its students and professors, is alert and aggressive. It has been the only force of considerable significance to attack the University Reform. In recent years, however, it has preferred to shelter itself within its own universities. It is sufficient to mention the creation of centers of higher Catholic learning in Guatemala, El Salvador, Buenos Aires, Cordoba, and Asunción, during the year 1960, to confirm what we are stating.

The Mission of the Latin American University

All this raises the main issue of the mission of the Latin American university. Our university, like others, fulfills its task deficiently. It is customary to say that the university is in crisis. The crisis is real but not surprising. The university, an institution that belongs to the historical world that we call the West, was born of a particular historical situation and has expressed over the years all the vicissitudes of that existence. The Latin American university is no exception. The fact is that no one yet knows just what the right answer will be to the present critical situation.

We feel that any reply must take into account the essential tasks of the university: those that are everywhere applicable, as well as those that concern our particular Latin American community. Among the first, we underline serving truth, searching for it diligently, and teaching it without a pause; exercising the creative intellectual life by means of vital contact with present problems; keeping teaching at a high level so that philosophy, history, physics, and biology are really taught and not just introduced, patchwork style; a real living together on the part of teachers and disciples and the influence of the intellectual excitement which that is bound to produce.

Together with this continuing work of the university are those tasks that correspond especially to our Latin American circumstances. These refer in the first place to the cultivation of living knowledge, and this has nothing to do with possession of a greater or lesser store of factual information. It has to do instead with the spontaneity and freshness with which we respond to things. We say this, reacting against

71

education understood as a simple heaping up of data or a reiterated management of formulas or predigested notions. Then, the Latin American university must stimulate research into the physical, social, and economic reality of our countries. Generally speaking, little research is being carried on and even that is in precarious condition. Another factor that weighs on the university is the exaggerated emphasis on certain professions like medicine, law, and engineering and the neglect of those that are being required more and more in our times, such as political science, sociology, and economics. Finally, the state university, which has been jealous of its autonomy, must not neglect its service to society. Through research and study it must contribute to the solution of the problems from which society suffers.

Christian Faith and the University

Why must the church take up the problem of the university? Is this a question belonging just to one age or is it that Christian theology has something to do with questions related to science and culture? Light is thrown on this question by remembering the attention paid by the Reformers to human problems, especially those of science and culture. Calvin declared in his *Treatise Against the Astrology Which Is Called Judicial* that the philosophers were not blind when they dealt with the secrets of nature; that those who invented medicine were not fools; that the scientific disciplines were very far from being a lot of nonsense. And he added: "No good science attacks the fear of God or the doctrine which He has given to lead us to life everlasting."

There is an attitude that tends to convert the Christian life into a purely subjective dimension, showing itself through the exercise of certain personal moral qualities. Questions of work and human relations remain unillumined by faith. Such a mystical Christian life ends by escaping from human conditions. The Biblical revelation shows that the being and

72

conduct of man gain in meaning when they are enveloped in creation as a whole and not confined in a pure individuality. This can be seen in the first chapters of Genesis where man is honored with a function of capital importance, that of giving names to things. This is not merely a formal naming but an essential function by which man reaches dominion over his particular surroundings.

We cannot attempt to close our eyes to the rupture that was produced between God and man through man's rebellion and fall. The human being has lost his sense of responsibility and of royalty, and the consequences of his mutiny may be seen in the anarchy and death around him. Yet, with it all, God continues to love the world. If "the wages of sin is death" (Rom. 6:23), the mercy of God desires "all men to be saved and to come to the knowledge of the truth." (1 Tim. 2:4) For that reason God preserves man and the world in existence in view of his redeeming purpose. The Bible, which speaks to us of the condemnation of man and his activity, witnesses also to man's privileged position in the world. Made a little lower than the angels, he has been crowned with glory and honor. (See Heb. 2:7)

Having as their object man and the whole creation, scientific activity and cultural life are expressions—very ambiguous it is true—of the position that man holds in the world and of the inalienable function with which he has been invested. That is why the university—a human community in which culture is conserved, created, and transmitted, and where scientific activity is developed and multiplied—is not a redoubt alien to the life of faith.

Scientific activity is a way of establishing relations with the world to mark out its quantitative and measurable aspects. The narrowing and reducing of knowledge to a certain order that the scientist effects, shows his desire to give the greatest objectivity to his work. For that reason he puts in parentheses all qualitative and value relations with the world that surrounds him. For him all intervention of the subjective is forbidden. Love and hate, desire and fear, aesthetic and ethical valuations remain as the forbidden subjective on the threshold of all scientific undertakings. To the extent to which the man of science has resolved to look at science from the objective point of view, he ignores anything related to sin and salvation, death and resurrection, the original and the new creation.

The Christian allows the investigator his right to recognize the realities of the world around him. The things he knows in the order of revelation do not claim to replace scientific research. The life of faith does not constitute a barrier to the life of science.

Culture is man's own world, which does not contradict the fact that man lives at the same time within nature and within or beneath the transcendent. Culture is humanization both in the process by which man becomes man and in the fact that the cultural products remain impregnated with humanity. Culture is basically, as Ortega y Gasset used to say, "a swimming movement," man's bracing himself against the sea of existence so as not to sink, a provisional place of refuge for his radical and constitutive insecurity. For that reason, culture is a testimony to human sufficiency and to man's unquenchable eagerness—always of course when he leaves out the realm of grace—to decide for himself and become his own God. It is this that makes it impossible to consider culture as spiritually neutral; its very grandeur and perfection, examples of which are not lacking, reveal a hidden guilt. Therefore, faith cannot accept it *in toto,* for within culture are seen the seeds of sin and rebellion.

The church, which alone knows what man really is in Jesus Christ, knows that man has not been created to revolve around himself and to reach divinity through his works, but to live in filial relation with God. There is no salvation by culture or by art, science, or technology. All cultural activity is affected by relativity and ambiguity, and it is God who will pronounce the final sentence on it.

Yet, this does not mean that we are to condemn wholesale the cultural expressions that have arisen from the secularizing process of the world. The sinner is still a man; divine grace does not allow him to fall below humanity. And even more, the church by means of Christians must be present in the painful nerve centers of our civilization to make itself felt where fundamental human values are at stake and there to give its testimony against every attempt to disfigure or to enslave man. Furthermore, culture, even that which ignores God, is preferable to barbarism. Culture at least allows for dialogue and in this way puts men in the presence of the gospel.

All that has been said refers also to the university. The preaching of the gospel is directed to the whole world and to man in the particular situation in which he finds himself. What mode does this preaching assume in the university surroundings? Let us understand here that besides pronouncing the name of Jesus Christ, the testimony of works is needed, that is, the dangerous effort to appropriate, rethink, and re-create from within, by means of the spirit of the gospel, the positive values of the age. This participation in the work of our contemporaries, which really involves the testimony of works, would be impossible with a theology of rupture that considers the world entirely bad and man's work as an absolute failure. It is possible, however, with a theology of reconciliation in which the Yes pronounced by God in Jesus Christ on the world surmounts the No that he pronounces with respect to our sin and self-righteousness. God's Yes in Jesus Christ, not the possibilities of the natural man, is the foundation of a positive attitude toward the world.

The guarantee that human work retains certain value, even within the situation of the Fall, does not reside in the sinner but in Jesus Christ. He makes the work of redemption cohere, as well as the work of man's continuous collaboration with man. Because of Jesus Christ, then, the Christian can take part in the work of men, to give a witness that is not one of eternal opposition but a testimony that recognizes all reasonable human initiative.

And this is the great task imposed on the witness of the gospel in Latin American universities, where an ideological pluralism with its confusion and unrest disputes the conscience. It is convenient, in an attempt to clear the ground, to distinguish three levels in all reading of history:[3] the technical history of humanity, the history of human experience, and the history of the Christian hope.

At the first level, the history of man is the history of work and the material and intellectual instruments of that work, of techniques and of institutions. At this level there is a continuous line of impersonal and anonymous progress if we ignore completely the concrete life of the individuals who suffer and desire, and the drama of the rise and fall of civilizations. Marxism is a useful hypothesis of work at this level. Christian faith may accept the intention—but not the pretension—and the optimistic reading of history on this level that Marxism makes. Man's vocation, according to the Scriptures, is to possess and cultivate the earth. But the gospel reminds us that while the exploitation of nature is permitted, the exploitation of man by man is sin and that the criterion of every technical undertaking must be, not the desire to dominate, but the desire to serve our fellowmen.

The history of human experience concerns individuals since every man must live his own life and, through certain concrete decisions, face alone his salvation and death. Existentialism calls our attention to the existential and mortal aspects of man's precarious situation in the world. Christianity may accept this reading of human experience, stressing life's ambiguity and man's responsibility to orient his life by his own decisions. The Christian, however, will not agree that man is the creator of his own values nor accept the absurd as the main plot of life.

Another dimension of history, foreign to Marxism and existentialism, is given by the hope of salvation in which the Christian enters into faith in the Lordship of Christ over history. The knowledge of the great acts of God in the world and in human history makes the church conscious of a hidden meaning behind the temporal succession of things and makes her trust that all events, whether of positive or negative valuation, are mysteriously guided or overruled by God until the coming of his kingdom. This mystery is open to faith; it is held in hope and therefore continues to be a mystery. God has spoken the definitive word in Jesus Christ. For that reason the church distrusts any system that claims to give a total and conclusive explanation of history, and whenever she must pronounce a word of condemnation it will be by the liberating and renewing word of the gospel.

Protestant Witness in the University

In general terms this is the situation that the Protestant student in Latin America must face in these days. The state university has been totally secularized. What attitude should the Christian assume in such a situation? In the first place, the preaching of the gospel, intended for all the world, is directed just as much to the secular university as to the Christian university. But the knowledge of faith can in no way replace scientific and cultural investigation. It cannot propose a method or hypothesis of work. When the church has tried to legislate in this field it has ended by ruining scientific investigation and by falsifying its message.

The student who is reconciled by Jesus Christ will use the same methods, proceed by the same analyses, share in the same relativity and discontinuity of human knowledge as the non-Christian. The scientific objects of his discipline will pass through the same test tube and miscroscope. The university Christian contends with science by putting into his scientific investigations the same resiliency and passionate curiosity as the university atheist. He knows that the work of God is the only absolute truth. On the plane of secondary truths, which is the plane of scientific study and research, he will be a witness pleasing to God if he begins by being as loyal and daring as the others in the venture to increase the progress of knowledge. Faith, without replacing investigation, shows the university worker his situation and reminds him that knowledge, besides being an offering to God, must be continually applied to the good of mankind.

Latin American universities are also centers of culture. Here the Christian revelation allows us to assume an attitude both cordial and reserved. We can appreciate culture in its ambiguity, but we must refuse its totalitarian pretensions.

The SCM in Our Universities

The process of secularization in our universities does not mean that Christ is despoiled of his lordship and exiled into other lands. God is working in our day in the Latin American universities. He does so, in part, through Roman Catholic groups, the Inter-Varsity Christian Fellowship, the YMCA, and through that Christian student community known as the Student Christian Movement.

The SCM is an evangelizing and ecumenical community, in nucleus Christian yet with open membership. Its goal is to proclaim the gospel in the university, together with the witness of works, and to offer students help in living as real disciples of Jesus within the life and mission of the church. By opening to all students the opportunity to study and discuss the problems that arise from their profession, from the internal life of the university, or from the natural and cultural circumstances in which they live, the SCM is placed in contact with many students who do not share, or are indifferent to, the Christian faith.

There are three important elements in the life of the SCM. The first and most important is evangelism. The SCM exists in the university principally to evangelize, that is, to make known the gospel of Jesus Christ. This evangelization is carried on through study, conferences, and discussions, as well as through the witness that each Christian gives with his life in the different professional schools. The second element in the life of the SCM is service in the church. The SCM does not seek to take the students from the church but to give them a sense of the importance of the church and its mission in the present world and to prepare them better to fulfill their responsibility. Finally, the SCM acts through the presence of its members in the movements and organizations of the universities and also projects its action outside the university on the social plane.

By means of international conferences, whether for the whole continent or for a region or country, the Federation and the SCM have shown their concern to deepen the claims of Christian vocation in the university; to bring the students of theology nearer to the problems of culture; to deepen the spiritual life of the people of God in our America; to help the students confront social questions.

A serious ecumenical concern runs through all this and presses the search for a form of united community life. Roman Catholic students participate in some groups, bringing added dimensions to the understanding of the ecumenical aspect of the missionary task. I believe that this ecumenical experience has been most useful, for it has strengthened the concern that students should come to be an active force in their churches, without requiring that they commit themselves to a particular denomination. In other words the SCMs do not intend to set up a kind of ecclesiastical selection, but simply to provide a spiritual ministry to students. It must be said that this is as yet a difficult battle in our area, not only due to all the hostile echoes caused by the mere mention of the name Roman Catholic, but also due to the presence of university Bible groups inspired by the Inter-Varsity Christian Fellowship. It has been hard to recognize with humble acceptance the fact of our divisions and to see the gift of unity that is given to us by the will of God.

There have been SCM groups that have carried on a fruitful task of exploration beyond the university world. There are those that have been concerned with avoiding every connotation that their group might represent an irresponsible elite. The work camp promoted by the SCM in Bolivia, in which the great majority of workers who participated were Indians, constituted a worthwhile effort to understand and reach out to a section of the population that has not as yet been completely integrated in the Bolivian community.

The theological and intellectual concerns evident among several groups indicate a growth in maturity that cannot be ignored. This is seen especially in Brazil, Uruguay, and Argentina, where ideological currents assert themselves vigorously. In the new Central American groups a concern can be noted for growth in spiritual life and the ethical implications of the gospel.

The SCMs in Latin America suffer many weaknesses and failures. The general attitude of our churches, which enclose themselves in a dangerous isolation, emphasizes the minority feeling of our students. The churches say little or nothing about the condition of the world in which they find themselves. The students, therefore, who enter the university suffer a sort of schizophrenia, in which their faith exists in a separate compartment with little evident implication for their work in the university or for later professional life. The lack of a serious grounding either in theology or in the life of the Latin American church means that the students find themselves helpless and incapable of action, unable to discover their responsible vocation in the world.

In the university, the SCM, uniting in one bundle different

temperaments and talents, is witnessing to the unity of all by the clarity of the word of some, the untiring action of others, and the style that some give to their life as students. It is true that the importance of individual witness is great, but each one is a member of the body and takes this corporate witness wherever he goes, and the body is vitalized by the force it communicates to the individual. In giving, it receives.

For the student world, this cohesion and lucid friendship are perhaps the more immediately discernible signs of the lordship of Christ in the university. "By this all men will know that you are my disciples, if you have love for one another." (John 13:35)

WALDO A.

CESAR

It was in Havana in 1946 that I decided to work entirely for the church, a decision until then hardly imagined. As a Brazilian, I was attending the Latin American Conference of Protestant Youth. One year later this decision was confirmed when I went, as leader of the Brazilian delegation, to the Second World Conference of Christian Youth, held in Oslo, Norway. These two occasions brought me an ecumenical vision and vital contact with work among youth in my own country. On returning from Oslo our delegation visited fifty-one cities in Brazil.

Not long afterward I was elected Executive Secretary of the Youth Department of the Evangelical Confederation of Brazil, a position in which I served until 1958. This work brought me into close touch with the situation of the church in all of Latin America.

Attending the Evanston Assembly of the World Council of Churches as a youth consultant, I had opportunity to discuss various proposals, principally regarding the need for studies about the social responsibility of the church and the need for both indigenous and mission churches to find more concrete ecumenical expression. From these discussions there developed the Studies on Rapid Social Change. At the present time I am a member of the executive group planning a Latin American conference to discuss the problems of church and society, which will be held in Lima, in July, 1961.

Three years ago I took part in the graduate course at the Ecumenical Institute at Bossey, near Geneva, Switzerland. Back in Rio de Janeiro, besides working in the field of church and society, I was named liaison person for Brazil of the Division of Inter-Church Aid and Service to Refugees of the World Council of Churches. Out of this work grew a new department in the Evangelical Confederation of Brazil, the Department of Immigration and Colonization.

At present, I am a candidate for the ministry, completing my studies in a special course of my presbytery in Brazil.

CHAPTER FIVE

THE CHURCH'S
TASK IN POLITICS

by Waldo A. Cesar

The first and perhaps most significant task of the Church of Jesus Christ in Latin America in the sphere of social responsibility is that of leading its members to participate actively in the political events of the present moment.

The importance and the influence of politics in a society in the process of change is unquestionable. Everything that is fundamental in such a society appears to depend upon decisions of a political nature. The progress of the industrial revolution, of agrarian reform, and even of education are subjected to the particular political leanings of those in power. The very concept of nationality itself is frequently shaped by party interests rather than technical and scientific concerns. It seems almost as though we ourselves are fashioned in the image and likeness of the state. If this predominance of secular power has any significance for the destiny of peoples, it is necessary that the church awaken.

The social task of the church would not be so urgent if we were living in normal times, if the needs and rights of citizens were guaranteed by the state within the limits of a kind of justice which made possible a life of plenty and security. If this were the case, the church could afford to limit itself to other matters: it could concern itself with evangelization based on the gospel of love and salvation and thus meet the basic individual needs of people. But when the social structures create problems whose dimensions seem to negate the very meaning of love, limiting it to pitiful and degrading alms-giving, sentimental compassion, or even indifference, it becomes necessary for the church to speak in prophetic tones so that the state may hear.

Fateful Choices

It is essential to take due account of the fact that the processes of rapid social change that are operating throughout Latin America indicate that we are now living in that moment which precedes the "great awakening" of which the economist Gunnar Myrdal has spoken.[4] Perhaps we are already awake. For what? Where are we going? There are forces demanding that we rid ourselves immediately of the domination of foreign power, whether this be economic, cultural, or political. All sorts of ideologies and "nationalisms" have arisen to express this secular revolt. A great tension has taken hold of all classes that are, to a greater or lesser degree, subjected to the dilemma of choosing between surrender to colonialism in the form of foreign economic domination, and revolt against it in nationalism. Such an option is today a matter for political decision of the highest importance.

Latin America is also awakening to the fact that the enormous rate of increase in her population, considered the most rapid in the world, will soon bring many problems which may profoundly affect her entire social structure. For instance, in fourteen Latin American countries considered in a United Nations study, only 1.7 per cent of the children of school age finish primary school. Yet even doubling the number of primary schools and teachers immediately would not improve this percentage but only barely maintain it, because of the rate of population growth. Also, if industrial expansion comes about in an era of inflation as part of the politics of nationalism, the fact is that the rate of industrial growth cannot keep pace with the population increase. This means that poverty will become even greater and that the state, through its political control and economic monopoly, will be confronted with incalculable social problems.

Some parties and governments have become aware of the acute contrast between poverty and illiteracy on the one hand and the inexhaustible riches of their land on the other. They have used this as a banner for their own demagogic battles for power. The demagogues know very well that the rural masses and those who have migrated from the interior to the astonishingly modern cities have no means to express their revolt and disappointment. These impoverished people are aware only that a new world is emerging and that industry promises them more even than they can now imagine in the miserable huts where they dwell, abandoned and apparently forgotten. In this situation, they are easy prey to the parties that seek power via the votes of the despairing.

In the midst of this panorama of social tension, what have been the spiritual forces that have tried to understand what is happening? What influence has the Roman Catholic Church, dominant during four centuries, or the Protestant church, implanted only a hundred years ago, been able to exercise? It is necessary to recognize that the relationship with social reality sustained by these two forces has not always been either right or appropriate. It is not that the church was absent, but its presence in many cases represented the negation of its true nature. Protestantism entered with its missionaries, but it was weakened through denominational divisions and had a certain incapacity to adapt since it represented a distant and supposedly "superior" culture. Roman Catholicism had established itself, partly by force, partly by the way it managed state-church relations.

Faith and Force

The common element in both Spanish and Portuguese colonization could be described by two words, ambition and faith. If it is hard to distinguish between these at times, the fact seems to be that ambition and the hunger for the possession of new land rather easily dominated the ideals of faith and evangelization. Pero Vaz Caminha, the chronicler of the expedition led by Pedro Alvares Cabral who discovered Brazil in the year 1500, says in his report to the King of Portugal that the land that had been discovered did not seem favorable for very much of anything and that probably the best fruit to be obtained would be the salvation of the people. Therefore, the first act of those who landed was to erect the cross of Christ before the savages. But the religious name first given to the new land, Holy Cross, was immediately replaced by a commercial name, Brazil, in view of the abundance of the wood that bore that name.

We must remember that this was also an era when great transformations were taking place. Geographical expansion and conquest, following the discovery of North and South America, marked the transition from the Middle Ages to the Renaissance. The Reformation and the Counter Reformation were in process. Feudal society was being transformed into bourgeois society. Capitalism was beginning to establish itself. And, in the midst of all this, religion cemented its relation with the state at every possible point and the king took possession of new territories in the name of God.

Perhaps it would not have been possible to achieve another sort of encounter between church and state, but the foundation of the error that today is being repeated was laid at that time. Because of the way in which the relationship between church and state was laid down, the church was involved in all the injustices of the state. When the lands began to yield economic advantages, the conquerors immediately started to torture and kill those natives who for any reason opposed their interests or would not submit to the work demands imposed upon them. In the case of Brazil, beginning in 1530, it became impossible to dominate and use the Indians to do the necessary work and there began the importation of Negroes from the Portuguese colonies of Africa. Thus slavery was introduced. The church then set out to evangelize the slaves.

And thus, like labor, religion was also something imposed. And because the church had not in any way become identified with the natives but had only been imposed, there began to appear that syncretic religion which to this day characterizes the Roman Catholic majority of Brazil and of Latin America in general.

Certain economic, political, and cultural characteristics that still predominate owe their origin to a disorderly and ambitious form of colonization. The church of the conquerors left its marks of superstition on the culture. A dualistic religion resulted, capable of separating the sacred from the secular and of maintaining, in these two spheres, special practices sometimes quite opposed to each other. Religion became in time a powerful political force.

Bread and Justice

The origin and the unfolding of the history of our colonization ought to be analyzed seriously by the churches. This initial impact of so-called Christian countries and rulers resulted in, paradoxically, a materialistic continent of perhaps the worst type. People mention God and his manifestations at all times and in all situations. But this God does not penetrate the social structures in which man is born, lives, and dies—without instruction, without home, without bread, and without justice. It is for this reason that the marginal sects multiply in Latin America. There are always masses ready to follow them even at great sacrifice. They are associated with the fundamental hopes of life. They promise bread, health, riches. Thus once again religion becomes mixed up with the state because this religion promises, by some sudden miracle, that which the state has not given except to a very privileged few or to those who make and carry out political policies.

Once again the encounter between the divine and the secular has become a blasphemy.

The literature of the continent provides several moving and, at the same time, startling examples of religious syncretisms and of the search for some miracle of economic redemption, of political and social salvation. The book of Euclides da Cunha, *Os Sertões,*[5] tells a classic true story of Antônio Conselheiro. He was a type of messiah to those who had nothing. He promised to give to his followers a new life. But his refuge in the jungles and his followers were destroyed to the last man by the armed forces of the government that feared the doctrine he preached.

The same false relation between faith and the social structure has, on the other hand, brought about the appearance of materialist ideologies. While the emotional appeal of the religions that promise miracles attracts the masses, those who are culturally more sophisticated are attracted by ideological formulations of Marxist origin. Some countries have tried their own brand of nationalism made up of various strains. *Aprismo,* the Apra[1] movement in Peru, for example, proclaims itself as a doctrine of social redemption for the whole continent.

In Brazil a small group of intellectuals have formed what they call the Higher Institute for Brazilian Studies. Though much attacked by the Roman Catholic Church, they have succeeded in obtaining financial aid from the government and are producing studies and giving courses to spread their "ideology of national development." The leaders of this movement say that it is necessary to understand national problems "in the context of a historical vision of the whole," interpreting these problems in terms of their universality. This group puts much emphasis on one point that is directly related to the problem of colonialism both in the past and the present. They say that Brazilians are not "authentic," that is, that we have not had a self-consciousness of our own. We have made use of the consciousness of others and as they have conceived us, so we have conceived ourselves. Thus we have surrendered the right to a point of view which is our own and have borrowed that of others.

It has been suggested that this is a phenomenon of colonial status. It is of the nature of a colony, some are saying, not to possess authentic self-perception but rather to be only an object in the thoughts of others and thus to conduct oneself as though one were an object.[6]

There is no doubt that the search for self, this affirmation of nationality so characteristic of the areas of rapid social change, only achieves balance and authenticity when the movement is thought through in terms of final deliverance from foreign economic or cultural domination, that is, from colonial status.

The Cuban revolution expresses this in drastic form. In his careful analysis of the Cuban question, Jean-Paul Sartre points out that "it is the beginning of the process of ending the colonial period for the whole continent."[7] The systematic revolt against dictators, which becomes ever more violent, is based on profound national feeling that will no longer tolerate the relationship these dictators have with foreign powers. In recent years various totalitarian governments have disappeared. A few months ago in the Bogotá Conference there was an expression of extreme discontent over the approval that the United States government has given to most, if not all, of the regimes that rule by force in Latin America. It was only after considerable pressure was brought to bear on the United States that the Organization of American States cut off diplomatic relations with the Dominican Republic.

An important question is appropriate here: What of the church? How has it reacted in relation to these situations that affect human life so profoundly? What is there for it to do in a continent that is feeling deeply the impact of rapid social transformation? If God is present in social and political events, it is imperative that the church witness to this presence not only in its worship but also in real encounter with secular forces. Without this the church will be irrelevant and will not be true to the Incarnation.

The role of the church cannot be limited merely to "talking against the world," of preaching against worldliness in fear of losing itself. In the place of merely verbal witness *(kerygma)*, it needs to identify itself in love *(koinonia)* and in service *(diakonia)*. Only thus will it discover the true dimensions of its evangelistic task.

Politics and God's Will

In reality, witness in a secularized society is far from easy. The social responsibility of the church cannot be expressed in terms of its relation to the state, unless we realize that this relationship involves the whole of society and all the specific aspects through which life manifests itself. It is from this fact that politics derives its tremendous importance, thus much that is done by groups and by individuals outside the political sphere becomes irrelevant. Principally this is because we are living in a society where the state is politically strong and orders all of the social and economic life. The basic directive that should guide Christians in their political relations is to try to help the state become the means through which God may carry out his plan for humanity. Our political participation should be based on the Biblical revelation of God's will for men. There is no other motivation that gives us authority as Christians to enter into politics; and this is sufficient to require that our witness be present there.

These basic considerations, which send us out to act in society, also offer us the means for constantly examining the way in which we exercise this ministry inside the existing social structures. In the first place, it is appropriate to remember that it is God himself who established governments and that his Word offers us the only valid criterion for judgment: "for in him all things were created, in heaven and on earth, visible and invisible, whether thrones or dominions or principalities or authorities—all things were created through him and for him." (Col. 1:16)

This suggests that the government is constituted in order to serve Christ and that, serving him, it also serves the church. Dietrich Bonhoeffer says that in guaranteeing justice and order, the government serves the church and makes it possible for her to live and to carry out her mission. He also affirms that it is the responsibility of the churches to testify before the government to their common Lord. The church must make it clear that in obedience to Jesus Christ the mission of the government will be fulfilled. Only the church can bring to the government the understanding of that which it is created to be. The church can never be silent on this subject. (From this we also reach the basic tenet that if the government opposes the church, the church should remain true to her Master.) Karl Barth is saying the same thing when he states that the existence of the Christian community, far from being non-political, is a political factor in the highest degree.

Once again it is Bonhoeffer who, in attempting to establish the basic elements in the relation between the government and its Lord, says that the church has the fundamental duty to preserve the world created by God. God exercises his power as Creator by means of two institutions that are prior to the state: marriage and work. The government receives these institutions and should maintain them. Through marriage the continuation of life is guaranteed; through work man maintains his life. Thus, whenever the government creates or allows political and social conditions that disfigure and perturb the full manifestation of these two realities that are fundamental to the nation itself, it falls to the church to make her prophetic voice heard.[8]

The church and the world have the same Lord. If the world does not know this, the church must continuously proclaim it. The church must be a permanent and even a disturbing challenge. It is a challenge evoking obedience to the Lord whom the world seeks in vain to forget.

Radical Engagement in the World

We must allow a certain realistic "intrusion" here, about the work of a divided, insensitive, and too often self-satisfied church. Without such an intrusion, we will not have the means to evaluate our position or to perceive the alienation and backwardness with which we are entering areas that are fundamental to human existence. Certain social and political movements, some of which are tinged with materialistic ideology, are God's judgment on the church. She has refused to run the risk of an encounter with the secular. Without such an encounter, however, there can be no redemption, only a ghetto whose comfort cannot last long.

A reassessment of the position we have inherited and which we maintain will come when the church allows herself to be permeated by the surrounding realities, so often understood better and more quickly by the children of darkness. The philosopher Michel Debrun makes clear the possibility—let us say the danger—that the relation between the spiritual life and the world will become "a relation of reciprocal limitations," that is, that each will become shut off from the other. The result of such a situation would be that the thought and language and, consequently, the action of the church would be mutilated and disfigured, taking on the point of view of an "imprisoned ideology," to use Debrun's term.[9] Worse still, the church is shutting the door to penetration by that other reality, the reality of Jesus Christ, which the world so desperately needs.

A secularized and materialistic continent, where politics is practically the center of all that happens, deserves a new and revolutionary effort on the part of the church—an effort at least as revolutionary as the political process that is operating in Latin America. This process is in rapid development. It affects not only the exterior life of man but, almost without his perceiving it, it is becoming the lord of his interior life as well. It is the task of the church to penetrate into this world of suffering and rebellion in order to proclaim the Reign that is to come. In order to do this she will have to accept the political and social consequences of the Incarnation, the most violent form of realism conceivable. In simple terms, the church will have to become engaged in the world and penetrate its political structures so that by means of them the demands of the supremacy and the lordship of Jesus Christ may be made manifest.

AHARON

SAPSEZIAN

Brazil is a country of immigrants, and the fusion of races and cultures is one of its marked characteristics. My own parents came from distant and historic Armenia, a name that calls to mind the tragic massacres at the beginning of this century, in which more than a million Armenians were exterminated simply because they were Christians living in non-Christian surroundings.

I began my theological studies in the Methodist seminary in São Paulo, with all the good and bad influences of a liberal education. The continuing problem for all of us, professors and students, was to discover how Christianity might become respected in the contemporary, technological world. Human culture was the criterion for the interpretation of the Word. How many of our efforts tasted bitter frustrations!

Near the end of the course, I and some of my companions began to read Emil Brunner and Reinhold Niebuhr. This was a release for us. We began to take the Word seriously, not so much in spite of its paradoxes, but because of them. With our concern about the integrity of the gospel, we began to be grasped by the necessity of its relevance. Relevance had a special meaning for us in Brazil. It meant the impact of the power of the gospel in a situation without precedent, where events were rapid and full of import, and problems a constant discouragement.

I spent one year at Union Theological Seminary in New York. There I studied with Reinhold Niebuhr, Paul Tillich, and John Bennett. In spite of their great differences, they were all Christians in dialogue with the world, though the topic of the day often varied. It is interesting how this concern with the world gave us a global comprehension of the faith that helped us transcend denominational limitations.

During my pastorate of five years, years in which I also taught courses at the seminary in São Paulo, it became increasingly clear to me that more important than the conventional piety and legalistic moralism of our Evangelical churches is the way we in Latin America live and interpret the gospel. Our faith must be characterized by a risking, prophetic attitude.

94

CHAPTER SIX

THE EMERGING SENSE OF NATIONAL IDENTITY

by Aharon Sapsezian

The social phenomena peculiar to our time and place force us at the very start to raise the issue of the church. By the express will of her Lord the church is placed *in the world*. It is here that she has her existence, and in principle she cannot evade this situation for it has been determined for her. Thus she must repeatedly be found at the vortex of the world's dynamism, in the clash of the forces and impulses that make up its history. Only when engaged, involved in the tensions of human events, taking history seriously, can she be faithful to her own vocation to live in the world. The church cannot deny this imperative to participate in the world. She can, however, tendentiously or thoughtlessly ignore it and make herself disgracefully marginal and irrelevant, while still conserving all of the apparatus of intense activism that is at base pseudo-historic if not quixotic.

What are the implications of the church's presence in the world? An important aspect of our responsibility as Christians is to stimulate serious, profound reflection in order to clarify these implications as far as possible and to live in awareness of them. As the church, we are called to give expression to our presence in the world in terms of the historical reality in which we find ourselves. This is one of the basic conditions of our authenticity as the church. The present national and international moment has for us Christians a double meaning. It is a tremendous challenge to manifest our relevance as the people of God in the face of boiling configurations of historical forces. And it is an opportunity, perhaps unprecedented, to make the creativity and vitality of our faith count in the formation of new and more fruitful social structures.

The church thus lives the present moment in obedience to her Lord who closes the door to escapism and to indifference concerning human events of social dimension. She lives it, too, with humility and contrition, because she knows herself to be responsibile for, and at times accessory to, the confusion and injustices of present history. She lives it, however, with determination and hope, in the certainty that she was called to be the manifestation and vehicle of God's love toward all men.

The Brazilian Reality

The term "Brazilian reality" has been used, at times, as a cliché to cloak with a mantle of erudition our incapacity to understand the complex of social, economic, and political phenomena that characterize our historical present. Nevertheless, we cannot abandon the expression; it serves at least to direct our attention to this constellation of facts, tendencies, and events that give a particular character to our present situation. Something of real importance is happening. We feel that the moment is decisive. If the many scientific, literary, and artistic productions are of doubtful value in interpreting the situation, they are nevertheless strongly expressive of this same reality. We sense, above all, that as the church we can no longer accept the condition of always being the last to know what is going on.

The complexity of the Brazilian situation, as that of the other Latin American countries, is more than obvious: it is manifest in the ambiguity and contradictory nature of the national ethos. On the one hand, there are signs of anxiety and perplexity that undermine confidence in traditional institutions. For they have failed to give man even a minimum of justice and security, which have become even more in-dispensable and vital in face of the rapid and profound trans-formations of our time. According to the pessimists we are galloping toward a chaotic, disintegrating collapse of all human values and of our own integrity as a nation.

Alongside this gloomy evaluation exists a compelling con-fidence in a "new world." Thanks to Latin America's in-exhaustible human and natural resources, it is believed that we are on the point of overcoming all our limitations in order to inaugurate the new era of prosperity and abundance, of law and justice, of integration and national dignity. For those who feel this way, all our difficulties are merely insignificant sub-products of the irreversible march toward a glorious dawn.

It is easy to see the deformations of these two views; however, one cannot deny the elements of truth that both contain. All of us participate in these two positions. Enthusi-asm and frustration alternately—and at times simultaneously —live in Brazilian hearts, as they do perhaps in those of our contemporaries in other parts of the world.

How is one to comprehend, then, what is happening? Do we Christians perchance have resources for understanding the complexity of phenomena that constitute the "Brazilian reality"? If we wish to witness and act in a relevant way— that is, if we want in fact to be present—this understanding is of basic importance. We should say at the outset that the simple fact of our being Christian does not give us any ad-vantage over non-Christians who are trying to understand the historical moment in which we live. It is very true that it is given us to see the facts in the perspective of their pur-pose, which is revealed to us; it is exactly this vision that constitutes the vocation and the service of the church in this case. In the evaluation of a determined, concrete histori-cal moment, however, we depend on research and reflective effort, which oftener than not are made by intellectual pioneers who have no obligations to the church. This means that an arrogant church that does not know how to enter into dialogue with the world's intellectuals and does not have the humility to learn from them is not in a position to know what is going on nor to live in a concrete situation.

Notwithstanding, we ought to add immediately that knowing our situation is not a purely intellectual task, much less an academic one. No reality of human life can be caught in scientifically objective concepts. If this is true for any intellectual, it is also true for us Christians. The Brazilian Evangelical church, for example, will come to know the national reality not alone through the quantity of study meetings she promotes, nor the number of erudite men she commissions to give opinions regarding problems, although such actions are indispensable. She will come to know it in proportion to the intensity with which she participates in this same reality. When she lives this reality with intimacy, in knowing herself she will know the world around her. It is in the capacity to become "all things to all men" that the church finds the ability to know the true significance and dimensions of a historical situation.

In any case, it is the church that must aspire, by the force of her vocation, to be found on the frontier of knowledge. Even though we do not have a final answer, even though we only vaguely glimpse the meaning of the events of our time and place, we must dare to throw ourselves into this task, not because we are sure of our virtues—their precarious quality is always in evidence—but because we act by faith in him who gave his Church the gift of *diakrisis,* the gift of discerning the spirits and powers that are operating among us.

The Evolution of a Sense of Nationality

The principal aspects of the present Brazilian reality point toward the "evolution of a sense of nationality." We will grasp better the multiple configuration of the economic, political, cultural, and social order of our country if we understand it along two lines: first, the recognition on the part of the nation of its unlimited possibilities of national integration and development; and second, its conscious determination to make these possibilities concrete. In reality this is little more than a working hypothesis to stimulate thought and to make possible more definite conclusions. However, we cannot ignore the facts that justify it.

To live in Brazil today is to live in the torrent of forces that are carrying out profound transformations in the living habits of human groups. The effect is similar, in part, in other Latin American countries and in some regions of Asia and Africa. The tendency of these forces is, first, to rouse the conviction that today we no longer have to accept underdevelopment, economic and cultural dependence, poverty, and injustice. We now know that certain audacious measures of restructuring our institutions can make the inexhaustible potentialities of the country more equitably accessible to all.

Second—and acting as a means to make the first conviction a reality—there is evident today an emphatic, unprecedented affirmation of the national values of Brazilian society with their integrating and consolidating power. There is the determination to defend these values from disintegration and exploitation in contact with other nationalities, and to put them at the service of the well-being of the people and of their search for identity as a nation.

We are in the midst of a dynamic evolution by which our nation is beginning to discover itself and sees, seductively within reach, the possibility of attaining its destiny and of creating more abundant conditions of life for many. The exaltation of national values and its use to fuse the aspirations and necessities of the nation and its people are the practical expressions of this dynamism.

It is useful to analyze from another perspective the nature of the forces active in this picture of events that we call "the evolution of a sense of nationality." As in all human history, there exists at this moment in our national history the action of controllable and uncontrollable forces or, if one prefers terminology more theological, destiny and freedom. We sense on the one hand that the situation in which we find ourselves as a nation is conditioned by certain factors that act independently of any conscious deliberation on our part and in the face of which there is little left for us to do but confirm their presence, tendencies, and effects. This means that we should understand the evolution of the sense of nationality within the context of a world-wide movement that has touched all those peoples who until now have lived totally or partially on the margin of history. This movement has been released through a new appreciation by peoples of their own identity and dignity. But on the other hand, it is exactly within this irrefutable mold of destiny that we also feel encouraged to exercise our freedom and our will. We sense that we can retard or hasten our evolution; reject traditional bonds and accept new ties in their place; create cities and move capitals; tame the immense, sleeping interior and subdue the vitality of nature; regiment new and vigorous political forces and give new directives to our education— all this by a sovereign fiat of our national will. Never has history let us feel ourselves such masters of our own destiny.

There is yet another important point that should be mentioned. The situation justifies once again the Christian affirmation that all human history is a permanent mixture of good and evil. We cannot, thus, neglect to characterize the demonic forces that are disputing the control of the situation and exercising an influence that does not promise well for the future. We wish to mention only some of these. Nationalism, when exclusivist and nearsighted, tends to reduce itself to a mystifying glorification of the national interest, giving it ideological sanction, but frequently hiding group interests. Progressivism, or what is coming to be known as developmentalism, induces

22800

us to believe in the redemptive capacity of economic and industrial dynamism, disregarding the other spheres of national life, and ends by thus justifying the constantly growing accumulation of wealth in the hands of a few. Political messianism, obviously the fruit of desperation, simplifies the complex social problem and naïvely localizes its solution in particular facts or individuals. There jumps to mind the danger of the ineptitude and the lack of realism of those who arbitrarily trace our destiny in terms of antagonistic alternatives, such as *entreguismo*[10] and nationalism, industrialization and agrarian policy, free and restricted international commerce, and other such slogans that thus obscure the multiple, more realistic possibilities that exist beyond these artificial alternatives. We cannot be silent; nor can we remain naïvely or comfortably inactive before these manifestations of evil.

It is a fact that there are demonic forces operating in history. But the great fact for us is that in Christ all these forces were definitively defeated. It is this faith that leads us to see creative and positive factors in this evolution of a sense of nationality. Exactly for this reason, we cannot fail to recognize the significance of the herculean effort of economic redemption. This effort is manifest in our foreign relations through the protection of the national resources from foreign exploitation and through measures to support the development of Brazilian industry. In domestic life this effort is seen in the anxiety for a more just participation in the fruits of the earth, for an economic as well as a political democracy. We cannot but stimulate the national policy that repudiates the conditioning of our national life by outside pressures foreign to our sovereignty. We see an authentic value in the tendency to progress beyond the phase of the coastal civilization, dependently turned toward other countries, and in the inauguration of national policies that centralize and integrate our country as we seek our own center and vital axis. Brasilia, our new capital city, for a number of reasons is the expressive symbol of this whole effort.

We also feel encouraged as we face the conscious pre-occupation of our intellectuals, artists, and writers, seeking to create a genuine culture emanating from our crucial questionings and perplexities and honestly turned toward our aspirations, necessities, problems, and hopes. These are signs of promise in the development of our nation. We have glimpsed new paths and feel impelled to enter upon them courageously in order to create conditions that permit a more fruitful expression of human life in this great country.

By these salutary signs, and above all by faith that the living God is sovereign over history, we cannot but affirm that Christ is present in the world-wide national and economic emergence of peoples and nations. We equally affirm that Christ is present in this moment in which our nation is awakening to the fact that it is a nation and is intrepidly assuming all the dangerous but necessary responsibilities of its vigil. The forces of the *aion* unchained in Christ are working redemptively despite the indifference, resistance, and even hostility of the defeated forces of the present world. God acts by the presence of his Spirit, who moves to create new, unpredictable configurations of life in anticipation and proclamation of the final manifestation of his kingdom.

The Vocation of the Church

If God is the Lord of history, then he is also the Lord of the history of Brazil and of all of Latin America, and let us say it with courage and faith. The church is called to proclaim this lordship, which is operating among us in acts of judgment and mercy. This means that we are called to be, in our time and place, the living proclamation of this lordship, and thus to be the eschatological community that discerns and lives out, by the grace of its resurrected Lord, the final restoration of all things. That is why we, as the Brazilian Evangelical church, although we can feel in the flesh all the frustrations and disillusionments of the present, can live in the rejoicing of final triumph. And if we can contemplate the national reality with fearlessness and hope, it is not ultimately because certain events and tendencies coincide with what we believe to be the will of God but because, above all, we know the powerful acts of God by which we ourselves were redeemed, and because we know that this same power continues to operate on all levels of life. God holds in his hands the reins of human history.

It is also in virtue of our faith that we can look with a certain humor at the false hopes of those who preach the millenium of a "new world" freed from its past and from the difficulties and anxieties inherent in this past. Evil is a permanent ingredient of human history; this fact permits us to affirm that even the new social and economic structures, created in the hope of eliminating old ills, already carry buried within themselves the seed of their own corruption. When old forms of unjust and demonic power have been dissolved, other unexpected and unpredictable forms will take their place, trying to continue their disintegrating work. Especially on the social scale, sin is surprisingly tenacious. Because of this, we as the people of God know that all historical facts are in the last analysis relative and precarious, as much in the problems they present as in the solutions that such problems by chance may come to have. We also know that our very presence as a church in history is in itself relative and has ultimate meaning only when it is understood as the precursor of the kingdom to which "the honor and glory of the nations" are to be returned.

And finally, it is because we believe that Christ is present in the social and economic phenomena which we observe, that we dare to speak of the presence of the church in the evolution of these phenomena. One can easily see, therefore, that we do it not because we think we have a panacea for the anguish of our homeland, or because we think ourselves capable of elaborating an idealistic plan whose functioning would guarantee general happiness, or because we have at our disposition any superhuman force to create a new order immune to evil. Nothing of the sort! We cannot attribute to ourselves such wisdom and power, for our own fragility is at every moment revealed to us in Christ. Our presence as a church requires something more serious: to respond with our total existence to God's action, which always precedes ours, and to accept even the ultimate consequences of the implications of our response. All our life, everything we do has meaning only when it is determined by our faith in what God has done and is doing.

One of the concrete signs of God's action in history is the existence of his historical church. We know that God's action does not restrict itself to the church; his Spirit transcends any frontier and operates redemptively in the world, although the world does not know it. Meanwhile, the importance of the church in this case resides in the fact that God chooses to act in a special way through her. Thus, as members of the Body of Christ, we cannot remain aloof from history. If Christ is present in the fundamental events of our time, then we will be concerned to be where he is. Our discipleship means that we must follow him in the paths of history. This is the fundamental content of our response to God's action.

We sense that this response demands of us certain decisions and courageous renouncements. The first of these is that we need to be in fact a contemporary community. We cannot continue to idolize our structures and ecclesiastical forms. Our strategy of action, mission, evangelization, and service in the world needs to be urgently rethought. Not infrequently we see ourselves confronting problems heretofore unseen, or new forms of old problems for which we are not by any stretch of the imagination prepared. Immense possibilities of more penetrating action are being lost because we lack the intuition of the importance and urgency of the moment.

Our churches, in the majority of cases, continue to be redoubts of men who judge themselves to be good men and who give themselves over to the refinement of looking at the world with arrogant compassion. Our pastoral work is often of a professional, routine, anachronistic quality; it is more concerned about serving the church than about bringing the church to serve God and the neighbor. Are, perchance, our programs of social action more than a comfortable tranquilizing alternative to our real social responsibility? What is there to say about our ironic disunity as churches in the midst of peoples who are seeking the highest expression of their unity as nations? In a word—if there is evolution in events, are we taking it seriously? Have we had the flexibility and dynamism to adapt ourselves to new situations, manifesting this readiness as a church in the flux of rapid, profound transformations? Are we, finally, meeting the new reality that is being delineated in Brazil, in Latin America, and in the world?

The second demand is that we translate God's love into the language of the turbulent and accelerated events of our generation. This love, whose mystery has been revealed to us, has repercussions in the collective social sphere in terms of an intense passion for justice. Theologically speaking, we would say that the absolute principle of love is the final and eschatological norm of our life, and its triumph an act of God. Still, as the beloved people of God, even in the ambiguities of history, we are called to act in defense of the structures of justice, which are, although relative in themselves, the social expression of love. Love does not rejoice at injustice. We who were touched by God's love cannot remain insensitive to the human aspirations for social, national, and international justice. To be present in the world, then, means to denounce patent forms of injustice and to unmask those that operate hiddenly; and, as the church, it means to support, increase, and strengthen the means and vehicles of justice that contribute to the true solidarity of the groups and classes which constitute the nation.

And above all, our presence in the evolution of the national events demands from us an attitude of sincere preoccupation in promoting an idea of the nation which, acting as integrator of the national character, can avoid on the other hand the risks of an idolatrous nationalism that sacrifices the individual and his inalienable liberty to the power of the state, and which refuses to recognize a superior level of a community of nations where all nationalism should find its limits. The fact that we are capable of seeing elements of worth in the nationalist ideologies of our time and our country does not authorize us to sanction them wholly, to the point of succumbing to the temptation of identifying the will of God with the interests of the nation. Without submitting to any ideology, Christians could well offer their irreplaceable contribution to the understanding of constructive nationalism which, conscious of its limitations and obligations, could be truly an agent of integration of the nation into the plan of God.

In conclusion, not only the Latin American nations, but the Evangelical churches in Latin America, are living in one of the most decisive moments of history. We as Evangelical Christians see ourselves facing an unprecedented opportunity to create a truly vital relationship with forces and events of national dimensions, an opportunity to be, better than we have been up till now, the salt that flavors, and thus to impregnate the life of the nation with a Christian concept of her destiny. We find ourselves at a crossroads that demands of us serious decision: either to keep ourselves on the periphery, superior, looking to ourselves, and thus irrelevant; or

106

to stop looking out for our own interests, giving ourselves, humiliating ourselves to meet the world where it is, in its social conflicts, its economic aspirations, its desire for justice, thus helping it to understand more clearly its relationship to the living God.

RICHARD

SHAULL

At present I am professor of theology in the Presbyterian seminary at Governador Valadares, on leave to serve as vice-president of the Instituto Mackenzie, which includes more than seven thousand students from primary to university level. It was begun by Protestant missionaries, still possesses something of a relationship with the Protestant movement, and is trying to discover what its vocation is in the new situation created by the rapid development of Brazil.

As a result of some years of involvement in the life and work of the church here, I am participating in the life of the Brazilian Student Christian Movement, the Department of Church and Society of the Evangelical Confederation of Brazil, and a number of other organizations related to the Protestant movement in this country. I also have the privilege of being engaged in dialogues with Roman Catholic leaders and of being related to several social and cultural movements in São Paulo.

What about the decisive events that have brought me here? The only thing to be said is that I have been led in directions I never planned to go and onto frontiers I never imagined existed. My wife and I went from the United States to Colombia as missionaries in 1942. There we engaged in many diverse activities in evangelism and the renewal of the church until we were transferred to Brazil ten years later. Here, we have found ourselves among a wonderful people with whom we are probably more at home than we could be anywhere else in the world, and called to share in the life of a country and a church where exciting things are happening—a country in a most dynamic phase of development in all areas of its life and a church living and growing, trying to find its selfhood and its mission in such a situation. It is here that I have been brought to face questions regarding what it means for Jesus Christ to take form in the Christian community and in the modern world. I am privileged to participate in a community engaged in this same search.

CHAPTER SEVEN | **NEW FORMS
OF CHURCH LIFE
IN A NEW SOCIETY**

by Richard Shaull

God has chosen to work in history through a special people. This people is the Body of Jesus Christ, through which he becomes visible in the world, is related to the life and problems of man, and carries forward his redemptive activity. Thus God's work in Latin America depends upon the continued development of a living and growing church that not only proclaims the gospel but also builds up the Christian community in which the Word takes on flesh and Christ is related to the hopes of men and the problems of a dynamic society. This raises the question of the forms of the church's life in the modern world. It is about the development of such forms within the concrete situation of Latin America today that the present chapter is concerned.

We shall attempt to show briefly how the rapid growth and impact of Protestantism in Latin America have been due, in no small degree, to the fact that a vital Christian faith was able to enter into a creative relationship with the life and problems of this continent and to take a form that responded to its needs. Then we shall proceed to indicate some of the elements that contribute to the development of a very different situation for the church here today and to examine the church's struggle to discover new forms of relevant Christian life and witness.

While this book deals with Latin America, the present chapter will refer almost exclusively to Brazil. This condition is imposed by the type of study we are making. Our aim is to examine the nature of God's work and of the church's response in our own specific situation, in the hope that in this way we will not only present a more vital and vivid picture of what is happening here but also invite the reader to re-examine his own situation and to engage in dialogue with the Christian community in this part of the world.

As this work is concerned primarily with the development of Protestantism, we cannot study Roman Catholicism except as its past failures and present efforts at renewal are related to the development of the Protestant church.

Early Heritage

It was Roman Catholicism that largely set the stage for the early development of the Evangelical movement. The Brazilian nation arose originally from three racial groups: the native Indian, the Portuguese colonizer, and the African slave. All three were baptized into the church, yet Brazilian Catholicism did not possess the resources necessary to transform profoundly the Brazilian soul. The church was weak; the intellectual, spiritual, and moral level of life of its priests was generally low, and Catholicism gradually became a social religion on the sugar plantations, which were the center of Brazilian life in the early centuries. There the superstitions of the Indian and the Negro not only continued but set the tone of the life of the church itself, producing a type of spirituality that was essentially syncretistic and lacking in vitality. With the impact of the French Enlightenment and the strong influence of Masonry and later of Positivism, the backwardness of the church was highlighted, and a strong anti-clerical spirit came to dominate much of Brazilian life.

The Brazilian people remained essentially a religious people, but their religious needs were largely unmet, and the few stirrings manifest in the Roman church were often more in the direction of Protestantism than of Catholicism as it developed in other parts of the world.

110

At the same time, upheavals were taking place in the social and political life of the country. New ideas of liberty, democracy, and enlightenment came from the United States and France. The more or less feudal rural society broke down, and new cities began to take the central place in the development of the country. With the end of slavery and the founding of the Republic, a new situation developed, which Roman Catholicism was unprepared to meet. Several of the more sensitive priests began reform movements that they hoped would lead to a renewed Catholicism, more or less independent of Rome, but their efforts did not succeed. The renewal for which they hoped was to come from a quite different source, from North American missionaries who arrived in the middle of the last century.

With the coming of the missionaries, a most unusual thing happened. This Anglo-Saxon Protestantism was better able to meet the needs of the Brazilian soul and to enter into a creative relationship with Brazilian national life and development than Roman Catholicism. Thus a strong Protestant movement arose with amazing rapidity, made a profound impact on Brazilian life, and brought about deep transformations. Because of its relevance to this situation, it appealed to people of all social classes, being equally strong among the poor illiterate peasants, the owners of the large *fazendas*,[11] and the intellectual and economic aristocracy of the new cities. Strong and growing churches developed across the country, and from the first decade an unusual number of capable and committed Brazilian leaders arose. Several examples of this creative relationship of Protestantism with the life of the people and the nation might be mentioned:

1. To a people religious by nature and tradition but dissatisfied and confused, Protestantism brought a warm evangelical faith, centering in a personal experience of Jesus Christ. Through the preaching of the Word, hymn singing, and Bible study, the rich emotional life of the Brazilian soul

111

was touched and transformed. The deep joy of Christian faith became a reality in the midst of problems and suffering. Bandits were converted; rural folk found new life in the midst of their monotonous existence; atheist intellectuals were overwhelmed by the truth of the gospel. A new type of spirituality and of human existence developed, which met the deepest needs of a people and exercised a strange attraction over those among whom the Protestants lived. It is this rich, joyful, and quite wholesome spiritual life that has impressed those who have come from other parts of the world and entered into a close relationship with Protestant communities in diverse parts of Brazil.

2. The Protestant church brought a new dimension and depth to community life on the plantations and in the smaller towns and cities. In these areas, stable natural communities existed in the nineteenth century, but they did not necessarily represent richness or depth of human relationships. Roman Catholicism was a strong force for social unity but it was not able to bring about a transformation in social relationships. With the establishment of Protestant congregations, such change was realized. Those who came to know the radical renewal of the gospel discovered that they belonged to each other in Jesus Christ. Thus a new type of human relationship developed in which the plantation owners or their sons in the cities and the ex-slaves were brothers in Christ, participating in a community of shared responsibility and engaging together in the work of evangelism. Here again a quality of life developed that was amazingly relevant to the human situation and constituted a powerful witness to the gospel in the local community.

3. The pattern of church life and missionary expansion that was adopted from the very beginning made rapid growth possible on vast and widely scattered frontiers. The early missionaries and pastors traveled widely, established small groups of laymen, and gave them authority to direct their

own congregational life and to carry on evangelistic work. The first priest to be converted by the earliest Presbyterian missionaries, José Manuel da Conceicao, spent the last years of his life wandering from village to village, stopping everywhere to read the Bible, preach, and teach. The missionaries gave a more rigid structure to this work but continued in the same direction. Thus a small group of believers in a local area would soon take on much of the character of a lay movement with all members participating actively in its life. On their own initiative they would begin "preaching points" or Sunday schools on neighboring plantations or in nearby towns, and, as families moved from one place to another in the vast hinterland, they gathered small groups of sympathizers around them, often hundreds of kilometers from any organized group or minister.

This same pattern has continued to the present time, although in some places it has lost some of its original spontaneity. Where Protestantism met a certain tendency toward a lay Christianity in Roman Catholicism, it added to it an expression and vitality that Catholicism itself was unable to provide.

4. The Protestant movement was able to relate itself in an unusually creative way to the new forces stirring in Brazilian life at the end of the nineteenth century. The Brazil of that period has often been referred to as a sleeping giant awakening from its slumber, becoming aware of itself and its potentialities, and seeking the foundations for a new way of life. Protestantism met this hope in a most relevant way. It not only provided a new ideal but also manifested the power of God to make the ideal a reality, by transforming the whole life of the individual convert and of his family. The gospel provided a new sense of moral integrity, a new seriousness of life and work. Children were nurtured in this transformed life, and every effort was made, often at great sacrifice, to provide them with an education. The local con-

gregation became a school in democracy and in responsibility, the like of which existed nowhere else in Brazilian life. The intellectuals who had felt the impact of new ideas related to democracy and freedom were easily led to send their children to Protestant schools and to support the Protestant cause. An unusual number of outstanding families in São Paulo and elsewhere were converted to Protestant Christianity in the early decades, and the number of leaders in national life who studied in Protestant schools as children and were profoundly influenced by them is even more impressive.

The Protestant churches had their weaknesses also, which are more evident now than formerly. They were too largely dominated by North American missionaries and influences; thus they preserved too much of a foreign flavor and failed to develop indigenous forms freely. As a few contemporary church leaders are now pointing out, the break with the Roman Catholic heritage in Christianity was unnecessarily sharp, and thus Protestantism often tended to alienate many of those who deeply felt the need for more vital Christian faith but who were unwilling to make the break demanded of them. Still, in the midst of these limitations, the Holy Spirit brought into existence throughout Brazil a strong Protestant community that has met the needs of large numbers of people and is making a profound impact on Brazilian life.

The New Challenge

The Brazil of 1960 is living in a new era, radically different from that in which the Protestant movement began. It is the Brazil of rapid social change, a dynamic society in which changes are so constant and radical that all the traditional structures of life and of society have been shaken and are being transformed. Industrialization and the use of technology have contributed to the exceedingly rapid growth of cities and have changed the ways of life of people, even in the interior regions. With the building of many roads in all directions across the country, areas formerly isolated and abandoned are suddenly feeling the influence of the outside world, while internal migrations have been speeded up in many different directions.

As a result of all this, many changes are taking place in the lives and attitudes of people. With the breakdown of the small, closely-knit natural communities, millions are now becoming lost in the rootless masses, isolated and abandoned in the large cities. With the cutting of the ties with the past and the overwhelming impact of the present, the distance between the generations becomes very great and creates acute problems. The older generation has lost much of its authority; youth tend to be impatient with all that belongs to the world of the past. At the same time, these same young people, in all of their revolt, often feel insecure and uncertain, for they have lost their confidence in past ways of understanding life and have not yet found other ways to take their place.

In more positive terms, the dynamic society has opened up new possibilities in almost all areas of life that now center upon the ideal of national development and fulfillment. As Brazilians become more aware of their own natural resources and of the tremendous opportunities that technology and industrialization open up, they not only become aware of the possibilities of overcoming hunger and poverty, but they also have a new vision of their own identity and destiny as a nation. This is the occasion for the centrality of nationalistic aspirations throughout Latin America as expressions of this search for national selfhood and of opposition to all those external forces, especially the economic and political power from North America, that threaten this independent development. Since this threat to national selfhood and a better life lies not only in outside power but also in the immensity of the internal problems, which are not easily solved, the intensity of the new dream has also created new tensions.

One more observation should be made. Although the Brazilian people are traditionally the most religious people in Latin America, the new mentality is overwhelmingly secular in character. Religion in Brazil has been associated with all those forces of reaction, backwardness, and injustice that are now being repudiated. Thus a new concern for human life and dignity sees religion as its adversary. The break with the past adds to this attitude toward religion, and the intensity of concern with problems of this world pushes religious preoccupations still further into the background.

In many ways, Brasilia is the symbol of this new mentality and new dynamic society. In three years a metropolis has arisen on a plain where nothing existed before. Modern highways go out from it in all directions across Brazil, and the whole interior region of a vast country has suddenly been opened up for development and tied to the administrative heart of the nation's life. Here is an amazing testimony to the reality of the Brazilian nation and what it can become.

At the same time, those who have been responsible for this development do not have an entirely easy conscience. To build Brasilia, it has been necessary to increase the poverty and insecurity of the masses and to produce an even larger number of uprooted people. Brasilia is a symbol of the complete break with the past that threatens us today. It has sprung up in an immense region that has had practically no past. It lives only in function of the present and the future. Its architectural design and total layout are in themselves a witness to this fact. Moreover, in Brasilia, we have a completely secularized expression of this tremendous drive to national development. It is said that the original layout of the city was in the form of a cross; it was finally constructed in the form of an airplane. All the lines of the major buildings are closed, thus giving no hint of any transcendent reality to which the national life is related. And as for visible manifestations of the church, they are practically absent.

New Forms of Church Life in a New Society

The Possibility of Relevance

All this does not necessarily imply that Protestantism is facing an impossible situation; in fact, there are many factors that open new and striking opportunities for the church, which did not exist in the static society of the past. But it is evident that the opportunities that lie before the church can be taken advantage of only to the degree that it is free to adapt to a radically new situation. Can this happen?

Protestantism has now one disadvantage it did not have one hundred years ago. Then, it was a new movement, free and flexible. Now, it has a century of development behind it and a pattern of church life that can become rigid, especially in the face of the insecurities and threats inevitable at this time. Then, the imported Protestantism was quite relevant to the situation of the moment as we have seen. Today, its possibility of relevance depends upon important modifications in its life.

At the same time, the Protestant movement in Brazil possesses certain advantages that may well put it in a unique position in the contemporary situation the church faces, not only in Brazil but in many other parts of the world. As one of the institutions of the present dynamic society, the Protestant church inevitably feels the impact of all these forces at work around it and thus is affected by them. In some other parts of the world, the pressures of society upon the church are toward conformity; here, on the contrary, the pressures on the church are in the direction of openness and change. As Protestantism is still comparatively young here, it does not possess the weight of tradition or the rigidity of pattern found in the churches of Europe or the United States. An unusual number of ministers and laymen, many of them in positions of leadership in the church, are aware of the demands of the present moment and are living on the frontier of thought and action. What is perhaps most important, the warm evangelical faith and vitality of the Protestant movement provide it with an inner dynamic, which can renew the forms of the church's life in the world and which, in the relatively flexible situation here, may bring about many new developments.

It is this that leads some of us to feel that we are in a rather unique position and that Brazilian Protestantism may be engaged in a search for expressions of church life and of missionary development that can be of significance for other parts of the world as well. It is this that gives a new dimension to the participation of the church here in the ecumenical movement. There is one thing, however, that must be borne in mind. At this point, in Brazil as elsewhere, we can expect no easy solutions to the problems we face. If the new situation demands radical changes, it is more important at this moment to understand clearly the problem before us and something of what it demands of us than to be able to produce easy answers.

Christian Experience and Worship

The Christian church in Brazil will have a vital and dynamic life and sustain its members in their witness on the frontiers around them to the degree that it is free to develop the forms of life that give adequate expression to the great realities of the gospel and of Christian experience in the contemporary situation. We have seen that the power of the Protestant movement has been due in no small degree to its ability to do this in the past, with its emphasis upon Bible study and a personal experience of Jesus Christ, which expressed itself in meaningful worship and in a rich devotional life, especially in the family. But as Brazilian life changes, new elements enter, demanding new religious expressions. The Brazilian church is now searching for these new expressions.

The crucial point is the nature of the believer's experience of the great realities of the faith. In the very insecure position in which he finds himself in a rapidly changing society, primary emphasis on subjective feeling no longer suffices. Christian experience must be set in the context determined by the great redemptive acts of God for man, which are the source of man's security and the fountain of his religious experience. Just as in the sixteenth century, the Reformation emphasis upon predestination, the sovereignty of God, and his initiative on man's behalf provided the foundation for dynamic living and action, so today a shift in this same direction is demanded. This is gradually taking place. Among groups of young people and university and seminary students, the discovery of this foundation has been a tremendous experience that has changed their whole attitude toward life and the world and provided a basis for dynamic growth in the faith.

Closely related to this is the search for more meaningful worship and richer sacramental life. Worship in earlier times was warmly emotional and led to deep spiritual satisfaction especially in the moments of strongest evangelistic emphasis. But as this worship has a very limited content, it tends to leave the Christian dissatisfied as the emotion of the evangelistic meeting declines. In this situation, there is much concern for a recovery of the richness of worship in which the great works of God are again presented and man responds to him in the totality of his being. Here the sacraments, as the visible expression of these realities and their significance for us, also take on new value.

It is not surprising that we are at present engaged in a search for more adequate patterns of worship. At the present moment, this manifests itself as dissatisfaction with what we have inherited and a longing, not yet entirely satisfied, for a richer and deeper worship. At the same time, interesting developments are taking place. Several leaders of the Methodist church are giving new form and content to their traditionally pietistic worship; in many Presbyterian churches, worship is receiving more attention; and in the Student Christian Movement there has been a great deal of group study of worship and efforts to develop more meaningful services.

A new interest is also evident in theology, with the possibility it offers of an integrative understanding of what God is doing in the world and in the life of men to illumine the human situation and provide a new basis for life and for action. Men and women are almost completely disoriented in the face of events in the modern world. This is the clue to the very real enthusiasm for theological studies that is evident among pastors and laymen throughout the church. They are engaging in group Bible study, reading books by leading American and European theologians, and organizing theological study groups. There can be no doubt that this has been of great help to many and is providing the foundation for creative thought and action for Christians in various areas of the nation's life.

Christian Community

The new situation forces the church to search for new expressions of Christian community life. In the early days the vitality of a warm Christian experience was intimately related to the fact that the local congregation was a closely knit Christian community in which its members shared an intimate and deep human relationship in Christ. This still continues in the rural areas and smaller towns of the interior. But today the trend is toward the development of large industrial centers, toward the rapid increase of population even in interior cities, toward extensive internal migrations, all of which tend to weaken or destroy the strong natural communities in which the Christian congregation formerly took shape.

As this change takes place, the program of church life to which we have been accustomed does not produce the same results. People who are totally isolated from one another in the large city do not automatically discover how to relate themselves to each other by attending several worship services or society meetings each week, nor are mere efforts to create fellowship very helpful. The gospel must build community where none exists; the church must discover how to make real for its members the new and deep relationship in a life of shared responsibility that Jesus Christ offers and of which we read in the first chapters of the Book of Acts.

In many places, and among a good number of people in the church, efforts are being made to discover what this demands. In a quite spontaneous way, this is happening in many city congregations as small groups come together, engage in evangelism, or participate in the life of the local young people's or women's societies. In some places, something similar to the house-church is taking shape. In many youth groups and among seminary students, the need for more adequate expressions of Christian community life is not only felt and discussed but is also leading to a new expression of solidarity and responsibility.

One of the striking responses to this need among the industrial proletariat is found in the Pentecostal churches. Here the workers who are completely alone and abandoned in the large city discover a sense of belonging and identity in a mass movement. Large crowds gather together each night of the week in a different part of the city for services of a highly emotional character. They not only are caught up in a great social movement but find that they have a place of importance and responsibility in it. There is no doubt that this has provided a real sense of belonging for people otherwise completely lost in the urban centers; whether it can offer a deep and enduring community relationship for them still remains to be seen.

There is a growing feeling among many that any real break-through at this point must come as a result of more radical changes in the community relationship of the local congregation. In some of the most advanced Roman Catholic parishes, this is being attempted through a new sort of association of Christian families. In a local parish a small group of families enter into a new relationship with each other, meet together to face their common problems, to study and worship together, and to share together the burdens of each member. In the student movement, attempts are being made to bring together, in this same sort of relationship, small nuclei of secondary and university students in the places where they study, and also to form similar groupings of men and women who are engaged in the same profession. In several instances, rather exciting things have happened in such groups, but no clear patterns have as yet developed, nor has it been possible to answer the question as to how the groups can become an integral part of local congregations. Here again, those most involved in these efforts feel that they are on a frontier where patience and trust are greatly needed as the Holy Spirit leads the church to the discovery of more adequate forms of community life and witness.

The Meaning of Ministry

One of the most distinctive characteristics of Brazilian Protestantism has been the very great emphasis on lay leadership, manifest from the start. In one Pentecostal group there is no clergy, and every layman has special responsibility. The older Protestant churches have not gone this far, but their vitality and growth is the result, to a large extent, of the strong lay participation in their life and work. With this also has come one danger, that of weak theological instruction and very limited efforts at Christian education.

In recent decades, the major Protestant denominations have tended to follow the patterns of their mother churches in Europe and America. Thus, each local congregation now wants a full-time pastor, who is often expected to do the work of the church. As this happens, the average layman plays an increasingly passive role and the congregation tends to become clerically minded. This trend becomes especially serious with the tremendous population growth, the extension of the cities, and the development of vast interior regions, for a church without strong lay leadership cannot possibly keep up with the task before it.

In the face of this challenge, there is a real concern evident in many places for the discovery of new forms of congregational life in which it will be possible to preserve some sort of order and authority and at the same time give the layman the maximum participation in the church's life and work.

There is a growing awareness that any progress at this point must be accompanied by new possibilities for intensive training of lay leadership. In the Presbyterian church this is expressed in the establishment of a new lay institute in Brasilia, the founding of a new seminary that is giving attention to this problem and to programs of lay training in presbyteries and local churches. In other denominations, similar developments are taking place.

Christian Life in the World

Brazilian Protestants have always been very much concerned about their witness in the world and have often lived sacrificially in obedience to this vocation. Today, however, this same seriousness of concern leads many to a certain sense of frustration. Witness in the world has usually been defined in terms of negative rules, which focus attention at points that are not necessarily the burning concerns of our time. To be primarily concerned about smoking, dancing, and keeping the Sabbath in a world in which there is so much revolution, suffering, and injustice, is not a striking witness to the relevance of the gospel to modern life. It is not easy to see the significance of the faith for the decisions the Christian must make daily in his professional life and in the society in which he lives. Thus the Christian is often uncertain and feels that his faith, if taken seriously, provides him with one more problem in a life already overburdened with frustrations.

At the same time, it is in the midst of this that many are coming to a new vision of the gospel. They are discovering that it is the Good News that the saving power and presence of Jesus Christ is a reality precisely in the center of their daily life and in the midst of the struggles and problems they face. Thus they are free to live dynamically in the world, discover a new style of life and commitment, and become involved in dynamic action in service to their neighbor and in the structures of modern society.

As they do so, they are often surprised by the miracles that daily occur around them and by the possibilities of Christian witness that open before them. Christian students get a new understanding of their purpose and responsibility in the university, become involved in student organizations and take a new interest in their colleagues. A group of young social service workers begins to discover rather unusual possibilities of service and witness to the Christian faith in the midst of their work; and quite a number of young men go into politics with a very deep concern for justice and for ministry to the needs of the masses.

Christian Unity

Visitors from Europe and North America are usually quite disturbed by the very strong denominationalism rampant here, and by the apparent lack of ecumenical concern among many in the Evangelical churches. It is wise, however, to attempt to understand this fact before judging too severely. The Protestant churches are all engaged in a tremendous evangelistic thrust on a vast missionary frontier. This endeavor absorbs their time and interest to the point that the more tranquil study of steps toward unity does not seem to be so pressing. Moreover, there is a suspicion that too much concern for the unity of the church or participation in the ecumenical movement might slow down this missionary drive by distracting attention from it or by leading the church members to conclude that evangelism is no longer necessary. Theological influences from abroad, it is often thought, might cut the nerve of mission. Equally important is the fact that the Brazilian churches, like the Brazilian nation, are searching for their own identity, trying to express their own life, no longer willing to be the reflection of an imported Christianity.

At the same time, the concern for the unity of the church is a very real force in Brazilian Protestantism. With renewed theological and Biblical study, we are coming to see that we are all members of one Body, that our unity in Christ is *given* by him and that we are called to make it real in all our relationships not only with our sister churches in this country but with the church of Christ around the world. Thus, many groups of young people and seminary students are engaging in study of the unity of the church and are searching for new expressions of it. Discussion goes on constantly about our relationships with each other in the Evangelical Confederation and in common projects and services. A great deal of progress has been made in this regard.

To discover how to express the unity that is given to us in Christ in this context is not easy. But the fact remains that it is in situations such as ours that new possibilities may open up for the ecumenical movement, for here the question of church unity is not a question of the study of the relationship between relatively static churches, but rather the discovery of how dynamic Christian communities, searching for their own identity as they engage in mission, can relate themselves to each other and be "one so that the world may believe." (John 17:21)

FOOTNOTES

1. The Apra, or Aprista, movement in Peru proclaims a doctrine of social redemption for the whole of Latin America. Its adherents look upon Latin America as a unit and they believe that the fundamental problems facing the republics can be solved by the adoption of the program set forth by the Apra movement. Its program, basically, calls for the people of Latin America to be themselves. To achieve this selfhood, the Apra movement supports control of imperialistic penetration of the area, unification of the area politically and economically, and nationalization of the wealth of Latin America. For a further development of the Apra movement see *Ideology and Program of the Peruvian Aprista Movement,* by Harry Kantor. Berkley, Calif.: University of California Press, 1953.

2. "The reformed university is being reformed."

3. Cf. *"Le Christianisme et le sens de l' histoire,"* in *Histoire et Vérité,* by Paul Ricoeur. Paris: Editions du Seuil, 1955, p. 80 ff.

4. Cf. *Economic Theory and Under-developed Regions,* by Gunnar Myrdal. London: Duckworth, 1957.

5. This book has been translated into English under the title, *Rebellion in the Backlands,* translation by Samuel Putnam. Chicago: University of Chicago Press, 1957.

6. Cf. *Ideologia e Desenvolvimento Nacional,* by Alvaro Vieira Pinto. Rio de Janeiro: Ministério da Educação e Cultura, Instituto Superior de Estudos Brasileiros, 1959, pp. 29-30.

7. Cf. *Furacão sôbre Cuba,* by Jean-Paul Sartre. Rio de Janeiro: Editôra do Autor, 1960, p. 10.

8. Cf. *Ethics,* by Dietrich Bonhoeffer, translated by Neville Horton Smith. New York: Macmillan, 1955.

9. *Ideologia e Realidade,* by Michel Debrun. Rio de Janeiro: Ministério da Educação e Cultura, Instituto Superior de Estudos Brasileiros, 1959, Chap. 4. Used by permission.

10. The selling out of national interests to foreign interests.

11. Large land holdings, estates, haciendas.

FORMAT NOTES

TYPE: 10 point Times Roman leaded 2 points.

COMPOSITION, PRINTING AND BINDING:
Sowers Printing Co., Lebanon, Pennsylvania

DESIGNERS: Format, Barbara M. Knox
Binding, Louise E. Jefferson